D1013290

The Spirit of
SERVANT-LEADERSHIP

Other Books by the Editors

Books by Larry C. Spears as Editor and Contributing Author

The Human Treatment of Human Beings (with Paul Davis), 2009

Scanlon EPIC Leadership: Where the Best Ideas Come Together (with Paul Davis), 2008

Practicing Servant-Leadership: Succeeding Through Trust, Bravery, and Forgiveness (with Michele Lawrence), 2004

The Servant-Leader Within: A Transformative Path (with Hamilton Beazley and Julie Beggs), 2003

Servant Leadership: A Journey into the Nature of Legitimate Power and Greatness (25th Anniversary Edition), 2002

Focus on Leadership: Servant-Leadership for the 21st Century (with Michele Lawrence), 2001

The Power of Servant-Leadership, 1998

Insights on Leadership: Service, Stewardship, Spirit, and Servant-Leadership, 1998

On Becoming a Servant-Leader (with Don M. Frick), 1996

Seeker and Servant (with Anne T. Fraker), 1996

Reflections on Leadership: How Robert K. Greenleaf's Theory of Servant-Leadership Influenced Today's Top Management Thinkers, 1995

Other Books as Contributing Author

The OnTarget Board Member: 8 Indisputable Behaviors, edited by M. Conduff, C. Gabanna, C. Raso, 2007

Robert K. Greenleaf: A Life of Servant Leadership, by Don M. Frick, 2004

Cutting Edge: Leadership 2000, edited by Barbara Kellerman and Larraine Matusak, 2000

Stone Soup for the World, edited by Marianne Larned, 1998

Leadership in a New Era, edited by John Renesch, 1994

Books by Shann Ray Ferch

America Masculine, 2010

Monographs by Shann Ray Ferch

Servant-Leadership, Restorative Justice, and Forgiveness (Voices of Servant-Leadership Series), 2000

Other Books as Contributing Author

Practicing Servant-Leadership: Succeeding Through Trust, Bravery, and Forgiveness (Larry Spears and Michele Lawrence), 2004

Journals Edited by Shann Ray Ferch and Larry C. Spears

The International Journal of Servant-Leadership, 2005–2009

What Others Say about Servant-Leadership

"Servant-leadership is now part of the vocabulary of enlightened leadership. Bob Greenleaf, along with other notables such as McGregor, Drucker, and Follett, has created a new thought-world of leadership that contains such virtues as growth, responsibility, and love."

Warren Bennis, Distinguished Professor,
Marshall School of Business,
University of Southern California; *On Leadership*

"I truly believe that servant-leadership has never been more applicable to the world of leadership than it is today."

Ken Blanchard, *The Heart of Leadership*

"We are each indebted to Greenleaf for bringing spirit and values into the workplace. His ideas will have enduring value for every generation of leaders."

Peter Block, *Stewardship*

"Anyone can be a servant-leader. Any one of us can take initiative; it doesn't require that we be appointed a leader; but it does require that we operate from moral authority. The spirit of servant-leadership is the spirit of moral authority."

Stephen R. Covey,
The 7 Habits of Highly Effective People

"The servant-leader is servant first. Becoming a servant-leader begins with the natural feeling that one wants to serve, to serve first."

Robert K. Greenleaf, *The Servant as Leader*

"With its deeper resonances in our spiritual traditions, Greenleaf reminds us that the essence of leadership is service, and therefore the welfare of people. Anchored in this way, we can distinguish between the tools of influence, persuasion, and power from the orienting values defining leadership to which these tools are applied."

Ronald Heifetz, *Leadership Without Easy Answers*

"The most difficult step, Greenleaf has written that any developing servant-leader must take, is to begin the personal journey toward wholeness and self-discovery."

Joseph Jaworski, *Synchronicity*

"Robert K. Greenleaf's work has struck a resonant chord in the minds and hearts of scholars and practitioners alike. His message lives through others, the true legacy of a servant-leader."

Jim Kouzes, *The Leadership Challenge*

"Robert Greenleaf takes us beyond cynicism and cheap tricks and simplified techniques into the heart of the matter, into the spiritual lives of those who lead."

Parker Palmer, *The Courage to Teach*

"Servant-leadership is more than a concept. As far as I'm concerned, it is a fact. I would simply define it by saying that any great leader, by which I also mean an ethical leader of any group, will see herself or himself primarily as a servant of that group and will act accordingly."

M. Scott Peck, *The Road Less Traveled*

"No one in the past 30 years has had a more profound impact on thinking about leadership than Robert Greenleaf. If we sought an objective measure of the quality of leadership available to society, there would be none better than the number of people reading and studying his writings."

Peter M. Senge, *The Fifth Discipline*

"Servant-leadership offers hope and wisdom for a new era in human development, and for the creation of better, more caring institutions."

Larry C. Spears, President and CEO,
The Spears Center for Servant-Leadership;
editor/contributing author, *Insights on Leadership*

"I believe that Greenleaf knew so much when he said the criterion of successful servant-leadership is that those we serve are healthier and wiser and freer and more autonomous, and perhaps they even loved our leadership so much that they also want to serve others."

Margaret Wheatley, *Leadership and the New Science*

"Despite all the buzz about modern leadership techniques, no one knows better than Greenleaf what really matters."

Working Woman Magazine

The Spirit of
SERVANT-LEADERSHIP

Edited by
Shann Ray Ferch and Larry C. Spears

PAULIST PRESS
New York/Mahwah, NJ

The Scripture quotations contained herein are from the New Revised Standard Version: Catholic Edition Copyright © 1989 and 1993, by the Division of Christian Education of the National Council of the Churches of Christ in the United States of America. Used by permission. All rights reserved.

Jacket back flap photo credits:
Larry C. Spears: Spotlight Photography
Shann Ray Ferch: Vanessa Kay

Jacket and book design by Lynn Else

Copyright © 2011 by The Spears Center for Servant-Leadership

All rights reserved. No part of this book may be reproduced or transmitted in any form or by any means, electronic or mechanical, including photocopying, recording, or by any information storage and retrieval system without permission in writing from the Publisher.

Library of Congress Cataloging-in-Publication Data

Robert K. Greenleaf Center. International Conference on Servant-Leadership (2005)
    The spirit of servant-leadership / edited by Shann Ray Ferch and Larry C. Spears.
        p. cm.
    Includes bibliographical references (p.   ) and index.
    ISBN 978-0-8091-0594-6 (alk. paper)
    1. Servant leadership. I. Ferch, Shann R. (Shann Ray), 1967– II. Spears, Larry C., 1955– III. Title.
    HM1261.R63 2011
    658.4´092—dc22

                                                                    2010030817

Published by Paulist Press
997 Macarthur Boulevard
Mahwah, New Jersey 07430

www.paulistpress.com

Printed and bound in the
United States of America

CONTENTS

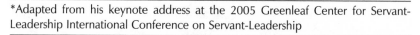

Foreword

SERVANT-LEADERSHIP: CREATING AN ALTERNATIVE FUTURE

*Peter Block**

*Adapted from his keynote address at the 2005 Greenleaf Center for Servant-Leadership International Conference on Servant-Leadership

I begin by paying special respect to Larry Spears' stewardship of the servant-leadership idea. He has managed to create a global network and bring the idea of servant-leadership into the world without commercializing it. In this modern day, that's quite a miracle.

Generally, when an idea is commercialized, it loses its substance and meaning. Once an idea gets popular and widely marketed, old binder covers are changed, and whatever was new in the idea is co-opted and lost. But Larry has sustained the spirit of servant-leadership despite its popularity. Partly this is because he has kept it vague and indefinable, which I think is a great strategic advantage. It is a conscious stance in support of the spirit of it, rather than the substance of it.

Robert K. Greenleaf was a model for me. It is not just the idea of servant-leadership that was compelling; it's that he valued thought. He valued thinking. He was a reflective human being. His commitment to reflection and discovery created the conditions for the shift in thinking that transformation requires. When people ask, "What's your life about now?" the answer is, "It's about trying to change my mind."

Modern culture doesn't value thinking; the world values *doing*. It wants to know *how*. How do we *do* this? Questions of methodology predominate. This culture worships the god of efficiency, the god of productivity. The questions everybody has are, "How do you make this work? How long does it take? How is it cheaper?" As if we could engineer our way into the future.

The thought that thoughts matter seems important. If there is something that symbolizes Greenleaf, it is that he was a thoughtful human being; he knew that an idea would change people's lives without specifying the form, nature, workshop, and materials that idea requires.

The question that servant-leadership raises is this: *What does it require to make a real difference in the world?* In other words, what is the nature of transformation? If we want to live in a world that authentic servant-leadership offers us, what will it take? Too many of my efforts at transformation have been mostly cosmetic, and the lip-service nature of the efforts is revealed by the questions I've always been asked: "How do we define the future you describe? And how do we measure it?"

I wrote an empowerment book years ago and a major soft drink company called me and said, "We like empowerment; it's become one of our core values. We've added it to our list of values: teamwork, customer, economics, community, and empowerment. Would you help us learn how to measure empowerment? Would you help us include empowerment in our performance appraisal program? Would you help us train for empowerment, so we know what it is and we know our people are getting it?" Those are all the signs to me of a cosmetic future. As soon as you start to go right to the practical, you say, well, this thing will pass too.

The challenge then is what is *truly enduring*? This is the question.

What would really transform the institutions that we work with? My most successful consultation was with Portland Gas & Electric. That's a place where I spent almost no time and they had huge changes. Most of my clients spend an extraordinary amount of time with very little change. PG&E was blessed with leadership that was truly interested in learning; they were in a crisis recovery from the Enron betrayal. They had a committed person in their training department, Scott Frank, who offered a three-day lateral leadership workshop that anyone could attend. It touched a nerve and slowly gained support and attention. The ideas in it had an impact. My only role was to support him in designing the workshop. My conclusion from this is that transformation has its best chance when it starts small, goes slow, and is very underfunded. Because the effort was low profile and peer-to-peer focused, Scott was able to build a community of support that finally gained some momentum. The power was also in the timing of the idea. When the culture is ripe, an idea can become embedded in community and something changes.

The heart of any effort at transformation is not the vision statement, but the way it is embodied. My own simple view is that vision becomes concrete in the way we bring people together. It is when we come together that the question of real change is on the line. Call this the nature of assembly and its capacity to give form to an alternative future. Assembly is simply the way we design our gatherings and the room in which we hold them. We don't have much consciousness about assembly. We still meet in hotel ballrooms, for example. We still meet in rooms that are unfriendly to community, that are unfriendly to aliveness.

The walls are blank in most of the rooms in which I work. The walls don't like that. I've been talking to walls lately, and they are very depressed when they have no aliveness on them. The wall says, "I went through a long process of framing, drywalling, painting, papering, and that was not to stand here and put up with no access to nature or have no art on me." The walls are that way. They often have no windows, so if you meet in a room with no windows you've just rendered nature obsolete. You say, "That's okay, Nature, we'll take it from here." How can we possibly create the experience of community, upon which servant-leadership depends, in an impersonal environment, in a modern, glass-and-steel-building society? The challenge is to inhabit our modern space in a way that brings aliveness into the room. This to me is the work. We cannot change the design of the room, but we can decide how to occupy it. How we occupy the space we inhabit determines whether we move toward a future like servant-leadership or just go through the motions.

It's one thing to sit in a chair; it is another to occupy it. This is what I have learned from improvisational theater. They say that once you stand in a place, then you occupy that space. You make a decision to occupy the space that you're in, which is another whole level of commitment than just standing there. The other thing improvisational theater teaches me is that when you're handed a line, you accept it. You don't turn it back. When somebody in improvisational theater says, "You're in a jungle; there's a snake four inches from your nose, and it's raining," you don't say to your improvisation partner, "I don't like that one. Could you send me something else?" This means to me that whatever life hands you, you must say, "How do I respond to what's handed to me?" instead of wishing or demanding or hoping that something else comes along.

What we are handed most of the time are rooms and cultures based on patriarchy, and we are trying to create service and community within that. There are certain things that are just a fact, and the patriarchal nature of the culture is a fact. Every room we walk into is typically organized for patriarchy. It's organized for presentation, display, PowerPoint® slides, and microphones. I know just what's going to happen when I walk into most rooms. It will be lined up for order, for efficiency, for amplification of one person over the people who are there to listen.

If my intention is to achieve transformation by building "servanthood" in this culture, then I have to rethink how we come together. This means I must continuously invert my thinking 180 degrees. One inversion is that the audience creates the performance. Maybe the listening creates the speaking. Maybe citizens create leaders, maybe employees create bosses, maybe students create teachers, and children create parents. Maybe the purpose for problem solving is to build relationships. In this culture, we think the purpose of relationships is to solve problems. You hear people say, "Well, we don't have to like each other to work together," which means, "Forget the relationship; as long as we get work done, I don't care who you are." These inversions are inherent in the servant-leadership idea.

The conventional thinking about leadership is that the speaker matters, the performer matters, the teacher matters, the boss is cause, my parents explain who I became. The thought that the person on top is the cause, however, is problematic. We need to invert boss-subordinate, teacher-student, parent-child, speaker-listener, and performer-audience.

Transformation thus hinges on where cause resides. You may say that's not true, the speaker does matter, the parent does matter, the teacher does matter, the performer does matter. I know they matter, but what would happen if I inverted this order, where would that take me? It's not an argument about whether the speaker or the listener is cause, but you say if I treated the listener as cause, where does that take me? Well, it takes me down a different path. In a conference, the worst thing that could happen is that the speaker would be good, for then when someone asked, "How was your first hour?" we would say, "It was great; the speaker was excellent." Then we would be in trouble because we would have to think that to have a great experience you'd have to have a great speaker. With this in mind, I've made a commitment to boring, dull, drawn out, and confusing keynote speeches, and I've built a reputation for that and I'm not going to give up on that easily. I won't be talked out of my mediocrity. It took me a long time even to reach this level. The gift in this is that if the audience had a good first hour even with a mediocre speaker, then they know they created the experience themselves.

The inversion of cause leads us back to caring about how we occupy a room, for every room we are in is a metaphor for the world. The room is the space where servant-leadership is embodied. For example, by changing the arrangement of a room we change how listening happens. The hardest place to create powerful listening, which drives the speaking, is an auditorium. It is a symbol of a patriarchal structure because if you want to move a chair you need a toolbox. This room is a ballroom. The chairs are lined up in rows to maximize attendance. A concession to the need for scale. One argument for this arrangement is that the fire marshal likes it this way. The fire marshal wants us lined up so we can exit quickly. If the fire marshals had their way, we'd meet outside.

This is called classroom style, all of us lined up in rows, and in tight places the chairs are locked to each other because they get lonely and so they need to embrace each other (I've personified all objects, including myself in a way). You say, "Well we don't want lines, let's do round tables." This is better, and then the next step would be no tables. How would you really create a room easy for occupation and habitation? You create a room with just chairs with wheels that swivel. The wheels mean I came here to move around. I didn't come here to stay in one place emotionally, spiritually, and intellectually. I need chairs that swivel because I want to look in all directions. I don't want to spend my morning with my friends turning their backs to me.

The point is that the way we assemble has enormous impact on who we become. The spirit of servant-leadership values the idea of placing leadership in the hands of citizens. It says that the action and the orientation are not where we thought they were; the cause is not where we thought it was. Every gathering has to embody this.

The qualifying question of transformation in service of servant-leadership is, "Do you want the future to be distinct from the past?" We have funny thoughts about the future and the past; we think we need to honor the past, we think we need to respect the past, remember the past. We think we have to learn from the past. The inversion in thinking is that none of these are useful; all of these keep me embedded in the past. What supports real change is our capacity to complete the past. Let me complete it. Let it be there and have it done; then that creates a space for an alternative future. If we are determined to respect the past, honor the past, and learn from the past, we end up being determined by the past. If we want to hold on to the past and do not want an alternative future, that's fine, but then what are we doing here? Let those wedded to the past find another room to be in. We want to be in *this* room where the future is waiting to be created.

The future is always created out of nothing. There's a void, a potential. Every time you have the courage to create an alternative future, you need that empty space, that space of potential. The reason I choose safety of conventional thinking—or conventional gathering—is that empty space frightens me. The reason I stay busy, the reason I now have my cell phone wired to my body, implanted in my body, is because I don't know what to do with empty space or silence.

In addition to how we gather and our willingness to keep the past in the past, servant-leadership also relies on the power of invitation over mandate. When it comes to bringing people into a culture of service, the only way the future is created in a distinct way is through invitation. The fulcrum for an alternative future is whether people are willing to exercise choice or not. Every step of the process needs to create space for choice. If we ask, "What's the work of transformation or creating a world that works for everybody?" the follow-up question is, "How do you confront people with their freedom?" It *only* happens through invitation. I'd rather have two people in the room who chose to be here than a thousand who were sent. And most of the places you work in, in organizations, people are sent. I always ask people, "Are you here by choice?" I ask groups, and they all sit with their arms crossed, in the middle-aged white male learning position, leaning back, as close to the door as possible. This too shall pass.

"How many chose to come?" I ask. In most workplaces, nobody moves. Then I say, "How many of you were sent or nominated for this session?" and they all raise their hand. I always wonder why they're so enthusiastic about their servitude; they could just casually raise their hand but they're waving emphatically. "I was sent and I'm proud of it." God forbid I should have made my own choices even in a small fashion, like coming to this meeting of my own volition.

The idea of invitation is central. What constitutes a powerful invitation? One that says, "Please come, and if you come here's what's required of you." Most invitations are too soft; there are elements of begging: "Please come, it's going to be great, nothing much will be required of you, it's not going to take long, we'll be fast, it'll be organized, Robert's Rules of Order, there'll be food, there'll be drink, the seats will be comfortable, and if you can come late, come at all, leave early, whatever, please come."

A powerful invitation is one that says, "We want you to come! Now if you choose to come, here's what will be demanded of you. You'll have to show up. You'll have to engage with your peers in meaningful conversations. You'll have to leave your interests at the door." We also require that people bring their imagination. We didn't come together to debate, or argue or express our opinions—that's not how the future is created. It is created through imagination. It's created from a dream. It is *possibility* that creates an alternative future. We're not coming to negotiate. Leave your interests at home. You're coming to engage in personal interactions between you and other citizens, other people. If you're willing to live by these requirements, please come.

To me that's a great invitation because then it gives you some traction with people. When you're working with the world you need traction, you need leverage. When people have chosen to show up, and they resist, you can say, kindly, "But if you are so filled with doubt, what are you doing here? What did you come here to create?" The idea of creation is powerful, but in reality it is hard to create. So choose only to be in rooms where people have come through invitation, even if it's just three people. So what is the strategy for transformation? Step one is to organize by invitation.

If you organize by invitation, then you pay the price of anxiety. The anxiety that nobody will show up. Especially working in the public sector. It takes you about a year to get up the nerve to make an invitation because we are afraid of people's choices.

In the private sector it is different. People come, but you are never quite sure when people say they came by choice whether they mean it. In the private sector, when people say, "Please come Friday at two o'clock" everybody comes. And if you say, "This is an invitation; don't come if you don't want to," everybody still comes. When they come you have to give them a second choice; you say, "Okay, thank you for coming; we're going to take a break in ten minutes, and if you come back after the break then you really want to be here." The idea is to pay great attention to the nature of the invitation.

I have talked about gatherings, inverted thinking, and invitation. Next is the power of questions. The future is given space when we postpone answers and even content. This is what I'm taking a stance for in the world, the postponement of content, answers, problem solving, and all the things we thought we came for. Instead we focus on connection. Building relationship and overcoming aloneness are the first orders of business. Each gathering should begin in small groups, in a circle, talking about something personal, like what they are committed to in the world, or what they came to this place for.

There is some risk in this postponement of debate and opinion. A sign of this is that in our culture you're not allowed to leave a meeting without a list. If you want to make people angry, say, "Welcome, we're meeting for two hours and we're going to leave here with no lists and no action plans. We are just going to develop our imagination." People get very mad. The argument, opinions, debate, and love of immediate problem solving are really a choice to avoid the demands of relatedness. When people do not value making contact with others a priority, when they do not want to invest in relatedness, then it is expressed by a demand for quick action, which is really a choice for nothing to change. The way quick action is postponed is through certain questions that focus on purpose, relatedness, doubt, and gifts. More on this later.

The spirit of servant-leadership also involves a conception of leadership that challenges the way leaders are currently subject to adoration. We need to drain away the enthusiasm people have for better leaders—to do so is an act of love, a manifestation of belief in the capacities of people themselves. To confront people with their freedom is to abandon the idea of role models. None of us is a role model, and that is a good thing. Which of us can claim that our way is the one to be imitated? I would recommend getting rid of the idea of the role model. Style is irrelevant and overrated. We do not need to change ourselves. We want to become more of who we are. The act of love, which confronts people with their freedom, is to assemble, invite, and lead, in a way that says the choice resides in all of us. What greater gift can you give somebody than the experience of their own power, the experience that they have the capacity to create the world?

Saying, "I will create an alternative future" is a declaration that I'm responsible for the world that I'm in. I've helped create the world in spite of the suffering I see in front of me or the leadership above. The opposite of this is blame, which is a covert wish for other people to change. Most of our public conversation is about blame. If you look at the media, it's all about finding fault with others. We don't care what actually happened, we don't care about the suffering, we just want to know whose fault it was. The public conversation is about retribution. The public conversation is the conversation held with more than three people in the room. Whether it's the media, the large community conversation, or our way of being together with three hundred people, our freedom requires that we change the nature of the public conversation. The way you do this is to confront people with the fact that they have choice over all this moment, which is how we come together.

Servant-leadership allows people to experience the act of creating something on their own. To create something, you have to be willing to tolerate the anxiety that comes with ambiguity. If you advocate servant-leadership, people are going to want you to define it. The wish for definition is the desire for safety even in the midst of adventure. You say, "I'm here to serve you," and they'll say, "What do you mean by that? Could you define exactly what your role is and what my role is in your service? What's expected of me? What do you have in mind for me?" My answer for that is to say, "I have nothing in mind for you." People feel abandoned when you do that. They want you to have something in mind for them, they want their Mommy, they want their mentor, and they want their performance review. That is what our interest in great leadership's all about—an escape from freedom.

"Leader, what do you have in mind for me?" The answer: "Nothing. I have nothing in mind for you. You are not someone I'm thinking about at night before I go to bed, and if I am thinking of you, it's not a good thing. Because the night is the hour of the wolf and I don't have kind thoughts in the hour of the wolf; they're dark thoughts, and so you don't want to be in another's mind between 2:30 and 4:15 at night."

The wish of people to be forefront in the mind of their leaders, and have their leaders "develop" them, is a wish for safety that is unfulfillable.

The point is this: you are pulling supports out from under people the moment you take servanthood seriously. It's not that the leader does not have a key role to play. Leaders have their own intention and possibility. The leader structures the engagement and names the debate. It is just that the leader need not have something in mind for others and does not exist to take uncertainty out of the future.

Let's return to the use of questions. At a very practical level, we confront people with their freedom through powerful questions that shift the locus of accountability to them. Servanthood requires excelling at questions that produce personal and collective accountability. Devise questions that, no matter how they are answered, bring out the responsibility of people as creators of the future.

Despite popular opinion, we can't *hold* each other accountable. We can't *legislate* accountability. We can do performance management, we can have rules of the road that we're going to enforce, we can talk about consequences; there have got to be consequences. All of these are forms of patriarchy and they have no power. They have no power to create an alternative future. They have no power in the world. The question is, "How do I engage people so they choose to be accountable?" Well, questions *do* that. There are certain questions that get you in trouble when you start answering them. No matter what you answer, you end up being responsible for creating an alternative future. The task of servant-leadership, in my mind, is to change the conversation, and to do it through small groups and questions.

The point is to be a convener of new conversations organized around questions that request citizens to be engaged with each other. And the questions have to be ones that have embedded within them the notion that choice resides in the world. It doesn't reside in leaders; it doesn't reside in any outside cause, fate included. Choice is not on stage with the performer, in the parent, in the teacher. Choice grows out of people's connectedness to each other, which is built through answering certain questions. Start collecting questions that produce the conversations that usher in transformation.

This presupposes that certain conversations have more power than others do. Most conversations have no power. Reporting has no power; explanations have no power. All my explanations are fiction. Even our hallowed stories about ourselves have no power because they are fiction. Certain facts happened in my life. I was born. I have evidence of that. My father died when I was fourteen. That's true. Most of the rest is fiction. I was abandoned, I felt bad, I was lonely, I was lost; all the explanations I have about my life to me are fiction; they're stories that I manufactured in order to ease the pain. That's disturbing in a way, but for me it's liberating. It means that if those stories are fiction, I can make up a new story any time I want. Therefore, explanation treats the story as if it's true. "Let me explain why I feel that way. Let me explain what got me here. Let me explain my history so I can in some way predict the future."

Reporting, explanations, analysis, opinions, community studies, summits, all those things have no power. They're interesting, and they give us something to talk about, but they have no power.

Here are some thoughts about conversations that have the power to create an alternative future. One is the conversation of *possibility*. What's the possibility I came here to live into or to create? Possibilities have to be unreachable. Most of us only set goals. I've worshiped too small a god in my life to be efficient, to be successful. The first half of life I just wanted to make a living, have a relationship that I could project onto, have a couple of kids that wouldn't be too hurt by the fact that my relationships have been a little volatile. Carl Jung says that what's true in the morning is a lie in the afternoon. What's true in the first half of my life is a lie in the second half of my life. And so the question of possibility is a great conversation.

There's a conversation of *ownership*. Take whatever you're complaining about and say, "What have I helped do to create that situation?" Beautiful question. "What's my contribution to the problem?" It means I'm an owner. Whatever I complain about let me turn that question and say, "How have I created that thing?"

There is a conversation of *commitment*. Commitment means, "What's the promise I'm willing to make with no expectation of return?" That's a commitment. Most of the commercial world, most of the living existing world, is organized around barter. What's in it for me? Entitlement. The side effect of patriarchy is entitlement. If you find people entitled, it's not who they really are. It's their response to a high-control world that has something in mind for them, and their contribution to that is the wish for safety and protection.

Commitment is a promise with no expectation of return, virtue as its own reward. The commitment question is simply,

"What's the promise you're willing to make with no expectation of return?"

Now, to whom do I make the promise? To *peers*. If you're in a leadership spot and you want to create choice, and you want the people working for you to be really engaged, then you have to let them make promises to each other. Let them sit in witness of those promises to peers, and have the peers ask, "If that person fulfills their promise, is that enough to meet our commitments to the larger body?" That shifts the focus from boss-to-subordinate, to peer-to-peer.

There's a conversation of *gifts*, an incredible conversation. Most of my life is organized around deficiencies. I'm deficiency-minded. I've been working on my deficiencies all my life, and I'm unfortunately working on the same deficiencies now as I was twenty-five years ago. That's how effective working on deficiencies is. For example, I have a small problem with finishing people's sentences. I don't know why, but when somebody starts to speak I always think, "I can finish this sentence, if not better than them, quicker than them." This may have something to do with arrogance, control, and self-centeredness. Perhaps. But again, those are just explanations. And so I've got this problem: I think I own the periods. I rent out commas, I rent out semicolons, I am in charge of when this sentence ends, and I will end it myself. I've been working on this for about twenty-five years with only marginal effectiveness.

Why do we still do a "needs analysis" (an organizational form of naming deficiencies)? Why do we still work on weaknesses? Why do we still give lectures on effective feedback? We teach that it has to be timed right, others have to be open to listening, and it has to be specific, concrete, and measurable. It's not about the person, it's about the action. We have people making a living on feedback methodology. And mostly the feedback we're thinking of is our disappointment in others, our wish to tell them about their deficiencies. Why package my disappointment in the label of feedback? People always come to me and say, "Peter, would you like some feedback?" I say, "No!" because I know that they're mad at me. Nobody expresses love by saying, "Peter, would you like some feedback?"—they just give it to you.

Suppose our primary purpose in leading would be to bring the gifts of the margin into the center. Suppose when we come together we agree for the next six months we're only going to talk about gifts. And we do it in the moment. We do it with each other and say, "You know, here's the gift I've gotten from you in the last ten minutes." And you teach people to breathe that in.

The elegant thing about these conversations is that any one will do. They all carry the same spirit, the same love, and the same willingness to surrender to the unpredictability of the future.

A final thought: we live in a world that values scarcity. Servant-leadership argues for a world of *abundance*. It's the economist who loves scarcity. For that world of commerce, it's great, but why should we let the economists define the nature of our way of being together?

Abundance creates a more human notion of what transformation toward servanthood really entails. What is reassuring is that all of this takes very little time. To change how we gather in a room, to invert our thinking, to complete our past, to create an alternative future through questions and a new conversation, only takes about ten minutes. How long does it take us to touch each other in some way? Ten minutes. So it's all a matter of design and intention. That to me is very hopeful.

Preface
SERVANT-LEADERSHIP: HEALING THE PERSON, HEALING THE WORLD

Shann Ray Ferch

What is the most central or ultimate image of human dignity?

Perhaps it is the smile of a child, or the loved one's embrace… or perhaps it is when we witness the grace of a kind word, or encounter forgiveness, or loyalty, or love. Birth and death attend us in a form of daily communion if we only draw back the veil a little and look with open eyes. Be it consolation or desolation, or the dynamic music of the living paradox they share, the contemporary world cries out with sacredness even as it reviles with profanity. Therefore, personal and collective discernment, or what Robert Greenleaf referred to as foresight, becomes paramount.

I believe when we hear the voices of leaders such as Martin Luther King, Jr., Corazon Aquino, and Viktor Frankl, we recognize the servant-leaders in our own life who loved us from the start, and without condition, and called us to what Lincoln referred to as "the better angels of our nature."[1] A grandfather, a sister, a mother, a brother, a friend—they drew us into a form of crucible. As our dross fell away they helped us rise, and we discovered in the encounter the timeless notion that perfect love casts out fear. This is a notion worthy to be given as a gift to our children.

So let us consider again the life of a child. What is it about a child's voice, a child's smiling face and exuberant laughter, that reminds us of the mystery and wonder of existence? Something of freedom is found in that smile, and peace, the simple, unburdened essence of being young and alive. Yet so often this essence is clouded in adulthood, becoming increasingly more elusive, and for some seemingly unreachable. At times our lives can be so filled with rapid motion, entanglements, pressure, and confusion we find it difficult to breathe.

We have fallen asleep and find ourselves caught in a nightmare. We wake to greater complexity and confusion.

What then can return us to a sense of clarity? At the core of servant-leadership is the uncommon and enduring notion of listening, even in the dark of our own difficulties. Deep listening. The etymology of "to listen" is "to obey." The root meaning invokes our obedience. Not to listen, in the original sense, meant to be absurd. And so to listen is an ultimate discovery of what is most worthy in life and in our relationships, and deserves our wholehearted response. Some things are worthy of ultimate obedience. Love. The beloved other. In the philosophy of Martin Luther King, Jr., echoing the words of Christ, even our enemies require an inspired and abiding love. A luxuriant love. Servant leaders are veterans of many wars, having entered conflict, suffering, and surrender, and emerged with hard-won victories. With great wisdom, the servant-leader carries a childlike faith and walks forward with courage.

Consider again the life of a child. There is something wonderful to be noticed in our children, something resilient, perhaps even invincible. I'm speaking of how they are so full of joy. It is difficult to find a depressed child, unless basic needs are not taken care of, and even then, their resilience is disarming. I remember a time when my first daughter was four years old. She was sleeping in our bed. She loves to get up early in the morning. I don't love to get up early in the morning. I like to sleep in the morning. That's gone now. But she loves to get up early in the morning, and you recognize that if a child is on your bed and stands up, she might walk a little bit close to the edge of the bed. It's a sixth sense with parents—even if we are half-asleep, there is a heightened awareness. We are always ready to grab her ankle if we need to, to keep her safe, to save her, to catch her, or to hold her. So she's walking kind of precariously on our bed on that day, it's pitch black, dark, and she leans over to the window. There are some Venetian blinds there and when she parts the blinds, sunlight pierces the room. She turns around and says in a loud voice, "It's a sunny day!" Just like that and I'm thinking, *Well I'm not ready for the sunny day. I want to sleep.* She walks back to the middle of the bed. It's June, the height of summer for us, very hot. December and winter are a long way off. She walks back to the middle of the bed and stands there. I have half an eye on her. She puts both hands in the air above her head and shouts in total happiness, "Christmas presents!"

She's like that. That's joy.

Now consider the counterpart to joy: despair. To live with the legitimate power involved in servant-leadership, not a power that dominates or controls, but a power that heals, restores, and reconciles, humility is necessary. The servant-leader submits to the subtle forces of life that lead away from self-embeddedness and toward the kind of transcendence that is capable of leading and healing the self and beloved others. Herman Hesse's elegant call in *The Journey to the East* gives a telling description of this process:

> Children live on one side of despair, the awakened on the other.[2]

Joy is a unique and courageous entity, a significant mover in our society, and one of the great engines of humanity. Earlier this year I had the honor of going to the Philippines to interview former President of the Philippines, Corazon "Cory" Aquino, a woman so filled with joy merely her presence brings joy to others. A couple of decades ago, only a few short years after her husband Ninoy's martyrdom, her spiritual, nonviolent, and love-imbued leadership rallied the great spirit of the Filipino people and toppled the Marcos regime. In many ways, I believe this set the stage for nonviolent movements that ensued in the following years, worldwide. Joy is something that Ninoy and Cory Aquino brought to the world—a great joy in the possibilities, the deep possibilities of life. Some things are worth fighting for. Our children, our joy, the fulfillment of a whole life—these are worth fighting for, which brings to mind the arresting and graceful sentence Ninoy uttered before returning to the Philippines from exile in the United States, only to be shot and killed immediately upon his arrival in Manila. The image of his body, dead on the tarmac, became a touchstone of justice and liberty for oppressed people everywhere. Before his arrival, before facing the death he imagined he might face, Ninoy said, "The Filipino is worth dying for."[3]

You see real joy in Ninoy and Cory Aquino. You see boldness and even the willingness to die so that others may have a better life. These are great dreams. Others too have generated great dreams. In America, Martin Luther King, Jr.—whom I would call a spiritual brother of President Aquino—also dreamed a great dream, and began to unseat the power abuses, privilege, and elitism that tend to surround circles of economic, political, and religious leadership in every society. Martin Luther King, Jr., a man of dignity for all people, led through service, action, and a resounding voice of strength, intelligence, and hope. He stated:

> Everyone can be great because everyone can serve. You only need a heart full of grace. A soul generated by love.[4]

Like Ninoy and Cory Aquino, and like Martin Luther King, Robert Greenleaf too was a person unafraid to dream a great dream; he is the founder of servant-leadership and his life and thought have richly influenced our ideas of leadership worldwide. One of the things we notice about America today is that Americans often consciously and unconsciously promote leadership that is egocentric, overly market- and consumer-driven, and harmful or even violent to ourselves and others. It is an area in which we need both much help and deep healing in our nation. Servant-leadership, from nation to nation, within nations, and internationally within our individual and communal lives, is drawing us to a better, more whole way of being.

Robert Greenleaf said:

> For something great to happen there must be a great dream. Behind every great achievement is a dreamer of great dreams.[5]

Consider Vincent Van Gogh, the meditative and vibrant iconoclast. He was not known for his art in his lifetime, yet one of his paintings recently sold for more than eighty million dollars. Though Van Gogh was a brave and deeply perceptive man, full of hope for the world and delight in God, he was also very troubled at times, and, in fact, he died in despair. Yet his truth lives on. He said:

There is nothing more truly artistic than to love people.[6]

Yes, the most challenging and true work of art is to love people.

Johann Sebastian Bach, the musician and composer, is another who was largely unknown. His music did not gain an audience until nearly a hundred years after his death. If one of us set out right now to script Bach's music, if we wrote down each note he wrote in his lifetime, it would take more than a decade. Because of this fluid and prolific quality and the unique nuances of his music, he is considered a genius. He could compose for orchestras in his head, the entire musical notation for every instrument, without even going to the piano.

George Frederic Handel was alienated, alone even in the midst of the great dream he dreamed. Consider this: he was at the bottom of his career, disrespected in society, dejected, living in obscurity, and at the low point of his life when a deep moment of grace came to him and he wrote the *Messiah*, the music that forms the glorious landscape of so many of our lives today.

My wife, Jennifer, read William Shirer's *The Rise and Fall of the Third Reich*, a scholarly and shocking book about Hitler's rise to power and then the tremendous fall. She has relayed to me so many accounts of people showing love and care for each other even in the face of the most atrocious conditions the Nazis had forced on them. Earlier this year, before I flew to the Philippines, she said to me, "You know, I believe it is possible for us to get better in chaos and suffering, and in difficulty, rather than getting worse." That's a profound sentence. That's something that heals me as a person just to hear her say it and heals our family just to have her as a part of our family saying it, living it. That we can get better in chaos, suffering, and difficulty, rather than getting worse; this is what Ninoy and Cory Aquino exemplify. This is what Martin Luther King, Jr., exemplifies. This is what Robert Greenleaf and servant-leadership exemplify.

In the leadership that rose from the Aquinos, Martin Luther King, and Robert Greenleaf, we see two significant qualities: deep spirituality and deep love. Their interior fortitude, the strength of their love for people, work, and life, is reflective of one of the vital truths from the scriptures of the Old Testament:

> Many waters cannot quench love. Love is stronger than death.[7]

Robert Greenleaf was a businessman in America who devoted himself to silence and to reflective quietness from his own spiritual tradition, the Quaker tradition, and out of that he started to form this idea of servant-leadership. His definition remains an important compass for all who desire to lead. He listened with awakened purpose. He spoke a lasting vision:

> The true test of a servant-leader is that others around the servant-leader become more wise, more free, more autonomous, more healthy and better able themselves to become servants. And the least privileged of the society are benefited or at least not further deprived.[8]

The servant-leader proceeds from within the heart of humanity, to heal the heart of humanity. The servant-leader is necessary. The servant-leader is good, and with deep conviction the servant-leader unknowingly becomes the antidote to the pernicious philosophies and ways of life that often accompany the interior world of family, organizations, and global relations, a world often preoccupied with the acquisition of power.

Marilynne Robinson's elegant and profound novel *Gilead* recently won the Pulitzer Prize. In rendering a character as whole as John Ames, Robinson imparted to America a much needed sense of spiritual origin, the life of the mind, and the intrinsic force of grace as a healing undercurrent to the nihilism and reductionist tendencies we so often and so unconsciously forward in the world. When *Gilead* is read in tandem with Robinson's *The Death of Adam*, the result is a crystalline image of the honor and dignity from which the human tradition of divine mystery arises. Her scathing rebuke of Darwin, Nietzsche, Marx, and Freud is worthy and resonant, and points out how a palate of nihilistic thought tips the world into objectification and cynicism, and a form of fortified atheism. She reveals the kind of rich discernment and robust mind, heart, and spirit that have given great service to the human community from the beginning. My wife asked me recently, what has been done in the name of atheism…what great efforts have arisen in the name of atheism? How does atheism engage the world's violence and poverty of spirit with an answer? The case can be made that the more militant forms of atheism often apparent today, just as in the work of Nietzsche and Freud, evoke an ego of the intellect that in effect not only precludes the heart and life of the servant-leader, but demeans and degrades the servant-leader, framing her or him as weak, ineffectual, and subservient.

Again, the question arises, how has atheism contributed to enduring personal and collective responsibility? Healthy skepticism, perhaps. Or perhaps a groundwork of cynicism toward the beliefs of humanity. That is, calling such beliefs into question, or demanding an accounting. To be sure, grave and inhuman hypocrisy has characterized people who believe in a "moral" universe, as some of the more vocal atheists in contemporary society are quick to point out. But the same hypocrisy haunts the atheist, yet without a living ideal or premise of human or divine value in which to place hope and action. Significantly, where action and hope join hands with integrity, the moral universe finds humble and profound resonance, as shown in the work of people such as Paulo Friere, Mother Teresa, Martin Luther King, Jr., William Wilberforce, Sojourner Truth, Frederick Douglass, Corazon Aquino, and César Chávez. From this legacy we find evidence, disciplined and sustained, of significant change in the human heart. In the wake of this change, a change redolent of human dignity, we see lasting contributions to the common good; to social, economic, and racial justice; and to the essence of what it means to be true and mature: *to love and serve others.*

Certainly, religious history is laced with human indignity and the abuse of people and power. Let it also be said that antireligious or irreligious history has its own dissuasive legacy. Consider the weight of the self-absorption and lack of respect for the connection between the human and the divine in the wake of leaders such as Pol Pot, Hitler, Stalin, Mao, as well as those who have furthered a similar legacy even in recent history in locations such as the Congo, Rwanda, and Darfur.

The pathway from life into life, and the complex and very painful passages that must be navigated, has accompanied the human project from the dawn of time. The more shortsighted we are, the less likely a compelling and sustainable vision will emerge to draw us to a better communal sense of ourselves. The more farsighted we are, the less capable we are to address the healing of the individual within the collective. An artistic sense of living helps us reconcile the polarities and gain a sense of persuasiveness with regard to some of the transcendent aspects of human existence: the true, the loving, the beautiful, the good, and that which is essential to being. In art as in life, the sacred can fall toward the sentimental. Through a nonrobust presentation of the world, the sacred becomes saccharine and loses the subtlety and force that accompany all great expressions of humanity. Not unlike this, the polar form in art and life is that which might be called the secular. In contemporary times, when the secular lacks discipline it ramps toward a profanity that not only goes unchecked, but is often exalted. The servant-leader is capable of holding in tension and with compassion the great paradox of humanity: the knowledge that we have within us not only the capacity for divine love, but for profane hatred. Therefore deep discernment, and the individual and collective action that rises from such discernment, is required.

When one of my three young daughters approaches me and crawls up into my lap and touches my face, I am reminded of the responsibility that has laid a claim on my life, a responsibility to love, and develop, and give of myself so that another life might become more wise, more free, more healthy, and better able to serve. My wife walks in dignity, and her voice illumines and makes whole the fragmentation so common to ordinary life. With her presence—confident, intelligent, courageous—she embodies a way of life inherent to the servant-leader: when confronted by life's ambiguity, injustice, or cruelty, the enduring legacy of true power asserts itself through wisdom, foresight, and healing. She sees what is necessary for wholeness. She walks forward and creates wholeness.

Viktor Frankl, the renowned psychiatrist and social critic who suffered the loss of his parents, his wife, and his brother in the death camps of Nazi Germany, believed in the integral importance not of seeking what we might gain or gather in life, but rather in seeking the answer to what life asks of us. In fulfilling life's deepest questions, in answering to life's deepest problems, meaning accompanies our way in the world and draws us to the true essence of the self and the beloved other. He believed we encounter meaning by creating a work or doing a deed, by experiencing goodness, truth, and beauty, by experiencing nature and culture, or by encountering another human being in the very uniqueness of this human being—specifically, by loving that person. Our personal approach to unavoidable suffering then becomes the crucible through which our humanity is honed and refined. Frankl gave us the following courageous statement regarding the call from life to greater life:

What is to give light must endure burning.[9]

Perhaps the most enduring image of human dignity is the sacrificial love given from one person to another, from one organization of people to the people served, or from nation to nation. Through love, by love, the servant-leader leaves a legacy of legitimate greatness and power. In this light, the kiss of a child, the kind word of a friend, and the fortitude that rests tyranny from the hands of the tyrant are one. In heart, mind, and spirit, the servant-leader not only sees us whole, undiminished, undestroyed, but also lives in such a way that we become whole. In so doing, we bring wholeness, or a sense of that which is holy, to the world.

In lives of those such as Aquino, King, Frankl, and Greenleaf, it becomes very clear that the core of courage and love is central to servant-leadership. The same courage, the same love is so evident in the beautiful essays that make up *The Spirit of Servant-Leadership*. I want to say how grateful I am to each author whose work appears here. Individually and collectively, their work points through the center of the human endeavor, into the interior, and from there out to the world. This anthology is designed to keep its finger on the pulse of servant-leadership socially, politically, economically, in science, in the scholarly fields, and foremost, in the heart of our humanity. I hope you find the work presented here enlightening, critically rich, and yes, full of joy!

The servant-leader lives a life of significance and others are drawn to their own great significance by being in the presence of the servant-leader. May a discerning love surround us in the pursuit of this great dream.

Shann Ray Ferch, PhD
Professor of Leadership
Doctoral Program in Leadership Studies
Gonzaga University

ACKNOWLEDGMENTS

Shann Ray Ferch:

I am so grateful for Jennifer, a fine woman who heals me and leads me to the best sense of affirmative life, for her soulful commitment to me and to our marriage. To Natalya, Ariana, and Isabella, our three daughters—may your lives be blessed with the garment of praise instead of the spirit of despair.

I also want to thank Paul McMahon at Paulist Press. Working with Paul has been a delight, and I am honored to see this manuscript find a home among the many profound and powerful books at Paulist.

Heather Veeder was invaluable in her service to this project. Her professional care and willing attention to detail are gifts to all those with whom she collaborates.

Finally, with gratitude for the friendship and the profound inspiration of heart, mind, and spirit, I thank Larry Spears. Our work together over the years has been a real gift and one of the central places of meaning and fulfillment for me with regard to servant-leadership and social action personally, organizationally, and globally. Larry's contributions as a thought-leader and a man of great depth of character have been an illuminating force behind the reach of servant-leadership throughout the world, and his quiet hope-filled presence has been wonderful in our collaborations at Gonzaga University and on so many vibrant writing projects.

Larry Spears:

I would like to offer special thanks to my family, friends, and colleagues around the world who have enriched my life for so many years, and especially to my wife, Beth Lafferty, and to our sons, James and Matthew Spears.

Thanks, too, for the support of The Spears Center Board (Council of Equals), including Stevens E. Brooks, Paul Davis, Kathleen Patterson, George SanFacon, and Lane Baldwin, and to all who have offered their encouragement and support for my work over the past twenty years—first at The Greenleaf Center and now at The Spears Center. Thanks, also, to the good folks connected to the Scanlon Leadership Network and Scanlon Foundation.

I am very appreciative of Gonzaga University (Spokane, WA) in so many ways. Among other things, it has been my great pleasure to discover how much I enjoy teaching several different graduate courses in servant-leadership for Gonzaga. Special thanks to G.U. faculty members and administrators: Mike Carey, Jack Horseman, Mary McFarland, and Shann Ferch.

I am particularly grateful to my colleague, friend, and coeditor Shann Ferch for many things, two of which I would like to mention here: In 2005 Shann and I began to collaborate on the annual *International Journal of Servant-Leadership*—a joint annual publication produced by Gonzaga University and The Spears Center. The *Journal* continues to break new ground with each passing year, and Shann has helped to make our collaboration on it a real joy over the years.

Second, of the dozen books that I have conceived and created over the years as editor or coeditor, this book (*The Spirit of Servant-Leadership*) has had an especially long gestation period. I actually began working on it in 2004, only to set it aside for several years while I worked on other books and activities. When I picked it back up again in 2008, I asked Shann if he would care to join me in moving forward with it, and he graciously said yes. Our collaboration on this volume since then has been full of good learning, encouragement, and productivity.

Finally, my sincere appreciation to servant-leaders around the world. You truly do help to keep hope alive.

TWO POEMS ON SOCIAL JUSTICE

Margaret Wheatley

I Want to Be a Ukrainian

When I come of age,
When I get over being a teen-ager
When I take my life seriously
When I grow up

   I want to be a Ukrainian.

When I come of age
I want to stand happily in the cold
for days beyond number,
no longer numb to what I need.

I want to hear my voice
rise loud and clear above
the icy fog, claiming myself.

> *It was day fifteen of the protest, and a woman standing next
> to her car was being interviewed. Her car had a rooster sit-
> ting on top of it. She said "We've woken up and we're not
> leaving till this rotten government is out." It is not recorded
> if the rooster crowed.*

When I get over being a teen-ager
when I no longer complain or accuse
when I stop blaming everybody else
when I take responsibility

I will have become a Ukrainian

> *The Yushchenko supporters carried bright orange banners
> which they waved vigorously on slim poles. Soon after the
> protests began, the government sent in thugs hoping to cre-
> ate violence. They also carried banners, but theirs were
> hung on heavy clubs that could double as weapons.*

When I take my life seriously
when I look directly at what's going on
when I know that the future doesn't change itself
that I must act

I will be a Ukrainian.

> *"Protest that endures," Wendell Berry said, "is moved by a
> hope far more modest than that of public success: namely,
> the hope of preserving qualities in one's own heart and
> spirit that would be destroyed by acquiescence.*

When I grow up and am known as a Ukrainian
I will move easily onto the streets
confident, insistent, happy to preserve the qualities
of my own heart and spirit.

In my maturity, I will be glad to teach you
the cost of acquiescence
the price of silence
the peril of retreat.

> *"Hope," said Vaclav Havel, "is not the conviction that some-
> thing will turn out well, but the certainty that something
> makes sense regardless of how it turns out."*

I will teach you all that I have learned
the strength of fearlessness
the peace of conviction
the strange source of hope

and I will die well, having been a Ukrainian.

The True Professional

The true professional is a person whose action points
beyond his or herself to that underlying reality, that
hidden wholeness, on which we all can rely.
—Parker Palmer

Illusion

Too much of our action is really reaction. Such doing
        does not flow from
free and independent hearts
but depends on external provocation.

Such doing does not flow
it depends on external provocation.

It does not come from our sense of
who we are and what we want to do, but from

our anxious reading of how others define us
    our anxious reading of how others define us
        our anxious reading of how others define us

and of what the world demands.

        When we react in this way we do not act
        humanly.

The true professional is one
who does not obscure grace
with illusions of technical prowess,
the true professional is one
who strips away all illusions to reveal

a reliable truth
a reliable truth in which
the human heart can rest.

Can rest.

Unveil the illusions
   unveil the illusions that
     masquerade
the illusions that masquerade
as reality and reveal
   the reality
   behind the masks.

   Catch the magician
deceiving us
   get a glimpse
     a glimpse of the
   truth behind the trick.

   A glimpse.

Contemplation happens anytime we get a glimpse of the
    truth.

Action

Action, like a sacrament,
is the visible form of an invisible spirit
an outward manifestation of
an inward power.

An expressive act is not to achieve a goal outside
    myself
but to express a conviction
a leading, a truth that is within me.

An expressive act is one taken
because if I did not
if I did not
if I did not take it
I would be denying
my own insight, gift, nature.

Action, like a sacrament, is the visible form of an
invisible spirit
an outward manifestation of
an inward power. But as we act,
we not only express what is in us
and help give shape to the world.

We also receive what is outside us
and we reshape
    our inner selves.

When we act, the world acts back.
The world acts back
and we and the world,
we and the world are

co-created.

    Right action is a process of birthing that cannot
        be forced
    but only followed.

Surrender

When God's love for the world pierces our armor of fear
it is an awesome experience of calling and accountability.
When God's love pierces our armor of fear
it is awesome
it is awesome to be pierced by God
to be called to accountability
to be called by God's love
for the world.

The true professional is one
who does not obscure grace
with illusions of technical prowess,
the true professional is one
who strips away all illusions to reveal

a reliable truth in which
the human heart can rest.

Reveal a reliable truth.

Let our human hearts rest.

This is a "found poem"—all phrases are taken from, i.e., found, in Parker Palmer's book The Active Life. *I then played with them and I hope extended them beyond Parker's original prose. I wrote this in tribute to Parker Palmer for the profound influence he's had on my work.*

Introduction

THE SPIRIT OF SERVANT-LEADERSHIP

*Larry C. Spears**

*President and CEO, The Larry C. Spears Center for Servant-Leadership

> The servant-leader is servant first. It begins with the natural feeling that one wants to serve. Then conscious choice brings one to aspire to lead. The best test is: do those served grow as persons; do they, while being served, become healthier, wiser, freer, more autonomous, more likely themselves to become servants?
>
> —Robert K. Greenleaf, *Servant Leadership*
> (Mahwah, NJ: Paulist Press, 2002), 27

Understanding Servant-Leadership

My dictionary offers the following definitions for the words *heart, mind*, and *spirit*:

Heart: *regarded as the seat of emotions, personality, attributes.*
Mind: *the thinking and perceiving part of consciousness.*
Spirit: *a pervading animating principle, essential, or character-*
    istic quality of life.

I believe that all three of these are important to understanding the essential nature of servant-leadership. Of these three, I believe that *spirit* is the one that is most noticeable by its presence in people and organizations. It is also the quality that is most noticeable by its absence in people and organizations.

The servant-leader concept continues to grow in its influence and impact. In fact, we have witnessed an unparalleled explosion of interest and practice of servant-leadership in the past fifteen years. In many ways, we can truly say that the times are only now beginning to catch up with Robert Greenleaf's visionary call to servant-leadership.

The idea of servant-leadership, now in its fifth decade as a concept bearing that name, continues to create a quiet revolution in workplaces around the world. This Introduction is intended to provide a broad overview of the growing influence this inspiring idea is having on people and their workplaces.

Today, in countless for-profit and not-for-profit organizations, we are seeing traditional, autocratic, and hierarchical modes of leadership yielding to a different way of working. It is based on teamwork and community. It seeks to involve others in decision-making, is strongly based in ethical and caring behavior, and is attempting to enhance the personal growth of workers while improving the caring and quality of our many institutions. This emerging approach to leadership and service is called *servant-leadership*.

We usually think of the words *servant* and *leader* as opposites. When two opposites are brought together in a creative and meaningful way, a paradox emerges. And so the words *servant* and *leader* have been brought together to create the paradoxical idea of servant-leadership. The basic idea of servant-leadership is both logical and intuitive. Since the time of the Industrial Revolution, managers have tended to view people as objects; institutions have considered workers as cogs within a machine. In the past few decades, we have witnessed a shift in that long-held view. Standard practices are rapidly shifting toward the ideas put forward by Robert Greenleaf, Stephen Covey, Peter Senge, Max DePree, Margaret Wheatley, Ken Blanchard, and many others who suggest that there is a better way to lead and manage our organizations. Robert Greenleaf's writings on the subject of servant-leadership helped to get this movement started, and his views have had a profound and growing effect on many.

Robert K. Greenleaf

> Despite all the buzz about modern leadership
> techniques, no one knows better than Greenleaf
> what really matters.
>> "The Best Books for New Bosses,"
>> *Working Woman*, March 1992

The term *servant-leadership* was first coined in a 1970 essay by Robert K. Greenleaf (1904–1990), entitled *The Servant as Leader*. Greenleaf, born in Terre Haute, Indiana, spent most of his organizational life in the field of management research, development, and education at AT&T. Following a forty-year career at AT&T, Greenleaf enjoyed a second career that lasted twenty-five years, during which he served as an influential consultant to a number of major institutions, including Ohio University, MIT, the Ford Foundation, the R. K. Mellon Foundation, the Mead Corporation, the American Foundation for Management Research, and the Lilly Endowment. In 1964, Greenleaf also founded the Center for Applied Ethics, which was renamed the Robert K. Greenleaf Center in 1985 and is now headquartered in Westfield, Indiana.

I was blessed to have known Bob Greenleaf, and to have served as president and CEO of the Greenleaf Center from 1990 to 2007. In 2008, I launched the Spears Center, where I continue to carry forward the idea of servant-leadership as first described by Greenleaf.

As a lifelong student of how things get done in organizations, Greenleaf distilled his observations in a series of essays and books on the theme of "The Servant as Leader"—the objective of which was to stimulate thought and action for building a better, more caring society.

The Servant as Leader Idea

The idea of the servant as leader came partly out of Greenleaf's half century of experience in working to shape large institutions. However, the event that crystallized Greenleaf's thinking came in the 1960s, when he read Hermann Hesse's short

9

novel *Journey to the East*—an account of a mythical journey by a group of people on a spiritual quest.

After reading this story, Greenleaf concluded that the central meaning of it was that the great leader is first experienced as a servant to others, and that this simple fact is central to his or her greatness. True leadership emerges from those whose primary motivation is a deep desire to help others.

In 1970, at the age of sixty-six, Greenleaf published *The Servant as Leader*, the first of a dozen essays and books on servant-leadership. Since that time, more than a half-million copies of his books and essays have been sold worldwide. Slowly but surely, Greenleaf's servant-leadership writings have made a deep, lasting impression on leaders, educators, and many others who are concerned with issues of leadership, management, service, and personal growth.

What Is Servant-Leadership?

In his works, Greenleaf discusses the need for a better approach to leadership, one that puts serving others—including employees, customers, and community—as the number one priority. Servant-leadership emphasizes increased service to others, a holistic approach to work, promoting a sense of community, and the sharing of power in decision making.

Who *is* a servant-leader? Greenleaf said that the servant-leader is one who is a servant first. In *The Servant as Leader* he wrote, "It begins with the natural feeling that one wants to serve, to serve first. Then conscious choice brings one to aspire to lead. The difference manifests itself in the care taken by the servant—first to make sure that other people's highest priority needs are being served. The best test is: Do those served grow as persons; do they, while being served, become healthier, wiser, freer, more autonomous, more likely themselves to become servants? Moreover, what is the effect on the least privileged in society? Will they benefit or at least not be further deprived?"

It is important to stress that servant-leadership is *not* a "quick-fix" approach. Nor is it something that can be quickly instilled within an institution. At its core, servant-leadership is a long-term, transformational approach to life and work—in essence, a way of being—that has the potential for creating positive change throughout our society.

Characteristics of the Servant-Leader

Servant-leadership deals with the reality of power in everyday life—its legitimacy, the ethical restraints upon it and the beneficial results that can be attained through the appropriate use of power.
—Alfonso A. Narvaez, "Robert K. Greenleaf, 86, Pioneer of Humanist Business Philosophy," *New York Times*, October 2, 1990

I have spent many years carefully considering Greenleaf's original writings, and from them I have extracted a set of ten characteristics of the servant-leader that I view as being of critical importance. The following characteristics are central to the development of servant-leaders:

Listening: Leaders have traditionally been valued for their communication and decision-making skills. While these are also important skills for the servant-leader, they need to be reinforced by a deep commitment to listening intently to others. The servant-leader seeks to identify the will of a group and helps clarify that will. He or she seeks to listen receptively to what is being said (and not said!). Listening also encompasses getting in touch with one's own inner voice and seeking to understand what one's body, spirit, and mind are communicating. Listening, coupled with regular periods of reflection, is essential to the growth of the servant-leader.

Empathy: The servant-leader strives to understand and empathize with others. People need to be accepted and recognized for their special and unique spirits. One assumes the good intentions of co-workers and does not reject them as people, even while refusing to accept their behavior or performance. The most successful servant-leaders are those who have become skilled empathetic listeners.

Healing: Learning to heal is a powerful force for transformation and integration. One of the great strengths of servant-leadership is the potential for healing one's self and others. Many people have broken spirits and have suffered from a variety of emotional hurts. Although this is a part of being human, servant-leaders recognize that they have an opportunity to "help make whole" those with whom they come in contact. In *The Servant as Leader* Greenleaf writes: "There is something subtle communicated to one who is being served and led if, implicit in the compact between servant-leader and led, is the understanding that the search for wholeness is something they share."

Awareness: General awareness, and especially self-awareness, strengthens the servant-leader. Making a commitment to foster awareness can be scary—you never know what you may discover. Awareness also aids one in understanding issues involving ethics and values. It lends itself to being able to view most situations from a more integrated, holistic position. As Greenleaf observed: "Awareness is not a giver of solace—it is just the opposite. It is a disturber and an awakener. Able leaders are usually sharply awake and reasonably disturbed. They are not seekers after solace. They have their own inner serenity."

Persuasion: Another characteristic of servant-leaders is a primary reliance on persuasion, rather than using one's positional authority, in making decisions within an organization. The servant-leader seeks to convince others, rather than coerce compliance. This particular element offers one of the clearest distinctions between the traditional authoritarian model and that of servant-leadership. The servant-leader is effective at building consensus within groups. This emphasis on persuasion over coercion probably has its roots within the beliefs of the Religious Society of Friends (Quakers), the denomination with which Robert Greenleaf himself was most closely allied.

Conceptualization: Servant-leaders seek to nurture their abilities to "dream great dreams." The ability to look at a problem (or an organization) from a conceptualizing perspective means that one must think beyond day-to-day realities. For many managers this characteristic requires discipline and practice. The traditional manager is focused on the need to achieve short-term operational goals. The manager who wishes also to be a servant-leader must stretch his or her thinking to encompass broader-based conceptual thinking. Within organizations, conceptualization is also the proper role of boards of trustees or directors. Unfortunately, boards can sometimes become involved in the day-to-day operations (something that should always be discouraged!) and fail to provide the visionary concept for an institution. Trustees need to be mostly conceptual in their orientation, staffs need to be mostly operational in their perspective, and the most effective CEOs and leaders probably need to develop both perspectives. Servant-leaders are called to seek a delicate balance between conceptual thinking and a day-to-day focused approach.

Foresight: Closely related to conceptualization, the ability to foresee the likely outcome of a situation is hard to define, but easy to identify. One knows it when one sees it. Foresight is a characteristic that enables the servant-leader to understand the lessons from the past, the realities of the present, and the likely consequences of a decision in the future. It is also deeply rooted within the intuitive mind. As such, one can conjecture that foresight is the one servant-leader characteristic with which one may be born. All other characteristics can be consciously developed. There has not been a great deal written on foresight. It remains a largely unexplored area in leadership studies, but one most deserving of careful attention.

Stewardship: Peter Block (author of *Stewardship* and *The Empowered Manager)* has defined stewardship as "holding something in trust for another." Robert Greenleaf's view of all institutions was one in which CEOs, staffs, and trustees all played significant roles in holding their institutions in trust for the greater good of society. Servant-leadership, like stewardship, assumes first a commitment to serving the needs of others. It also emphasizes the use of openness and persuasion rather than control.

Commitment to the growth of people: Servant-leaders believe that people have an intrinsic value beyond their tangible contributions as workers. As such, the servant-leader is deeply committed to the growth of every individual within his or her institution. The servant-leader recognizes the tremendous responsibility to do everything within his or her power to nurture the personal, professional, and spiritual growth of employees. In practice, this can include (but is not limited to) concrete actions such as making available funds for personal and professional development, taking a personal interest in the ideas and suggestions from everyone, encouraging worker involvement in decision making, and actively assisting laid-off workers to find other employment.

Building community: The servant-leader senses that much has been lost in recent human history because of the shift from local communities to large institutions as the primary shapers of human lives. This awareness causes the servant-leader to seek to identify some means for building community among those who work within a given institution. Servant-leadership suggests that true community can be created among those who work in businesses and other institutions. Greenleaf said, "All that is needed to rebuild community as a viable life form for large numbers of people is for enough servant-leaders to show the way, not by mass movements, but by each servant-leader demonstrating his own unlimited liability for a quite specific community-related group."

These ten characteristics of servant-leadership are by no means exhaustive. However, I believe that the ones listed serve to communicate the power and promise that this concept offers to those who are open to its invitation and challenge.

Servant-Leadership in Practice

Servant-leadership has emerged as one of the dominant philosophies being discussed in the world today.
—Larry C. Spears, "Servant Leadership Grows in Acceptance," *Indianapolis Business Journal* (September 4–10, 1995): 24.

1. Servant-Leadership as an Institutional Model

Servant-leadership principles are being applied in significant ways in many different areas. The first area has to do with servant-leadership as an institutional philosophy and model. Servant-leadership crosses all boundaries and is being applied by a wide variety of people working with for-profit businesses; not-for-profit corporations; and churches, universities, healthcare institutions, and foundations.

Servant-leadership advocates a group-oriented approach to analysis and decision making as a means of strengthening institutions and improving society. It also emphasizes the power of persuasion and seeking consensus, over the old top-down form of leadership. Some people have likened this to turning the hierarchical pyramid upside down. Servant-leadership holds that the primary purpose of a business should be to create a positive impact on its employees and community, rather than using profit as the sole motive.

Many individuals within institutions have adopted servant-leadership as a guiding philosophy. An increasing number of companies have adopted servant-leadership as part of their corporate philosophy or as a foundation for their mission statement. Among these are Toro (Minneapolis, Minnesota), Synovus Financial (Columbus, Georgia), ServiceMaster (Downers Grove, Illinois), the Men's Wearhouse (Fremont, California), Southwest Airlines (Dallas, Texas), and TDIndustries (Dallas, Texas).

TDIndustries (TD), one of the earliest practitioners of servant-leadership in the corporate setting, is a Dallas-based heating and plumbing contracting firm that has consistently ranked in the top ten of *Fortune's* "100 Best Companies to Work for in America." TD's founder, Jack Lowe, Sr., came upon *The Servant as Leader* essay in the early 1970s and began to distribute copies of it to his employees. They were invited to read the essay and then to gather in small groups to discuss its meaning. The belief that managers should serve their employees became an important value for TDIndustries.

Thirty-five years later, TDIndustries continues to use servant-leadership as its guiding philosophy. Even today, any TDPartner who supervises at least one person must go through training in servant-leadership. In addition, all new employees continue to receive a copy of *The Servant as Leader* essay; and TD has developed elaborate training modules designed to encourage the understanding and practice of servant-leadership.

Some businesses have begun to view servant-leadership as an important framework that is helpful (and necessary) for ensuring the long-term effects of related management and leadership approaches such as continuous quality improvement and systems thinking. It is suggested that institutions that want to create meaningful change may be best served in starting with servant-leadership as the foundational understanding and then building on it through any number of related approaches.

Servant-leadership has influenced many noted writers, thinkers, and leaders. Max DePree, former chair of the Herman Miller Company, has said, "The servanthood of leadership needs to be felt, understood, believed, and practiced" (Max DePree, *Leadership Jazz* [New York: Doubleday, 1992], 8). In addition, Peter Senge has said that he tells people "not to bother reading any other book about leadership until you first read Robert Greenleaf's book, *Servant-Leadership*. I believe it is the most singular and useful statement on leadership I've come across" (Peter Senge, Greenleaf Center Conference presentation, Indianapolis, 1992). In recent years, a growing number of leaders and readers have "rediscovered" Robert Greenleaf's own writings through books by DePree, Senge, Covey, Wheatley, Autry, and many other popular writers.

2. Education and Training of Not-for-Profit Trustees

A second major application of servant-leadership is its pivotal role as the theoretical and ethical basis for "trustee education." Greenleaf wrote extensively on servant-leadership as it applies to the roles of boards of directors and trustees within institutions. His essays on these applications are widely distributed among directors of for-profit and nonprofit organizations. In his essay, "Trustees as Servants," Greenleaf urged trustees to ask themselves two central questions: "Whom do you serve?" and "For what purpose?"

Servant-leadership suggests that boards of trustees need to undergo a radical shift in how they approach their roles. Trustees who seek to act as servant-leaders can help to create institutions of great depth and quality. Over the past decade, two of America's largest grant-making foundations (the Lilly Endowment and the W. K. Kellogg Foundation) have sought to encourage the development of programs designed to educate and train not-for-profit boards of trustees to function as servant-leaders. John Carver, the noted author on board governance, has also done much to raise awareness of servant-leadership in relation to trustee boards.

3. *Community Leadership Programs*

A third application of servant-leadership concerns its deepening role in community leadership organizations across the country. A growing number of community leadership groups are using Greenleaf Center resources as part of their own education and training efforts. Some have been doing so for more than twenty years.

M. Scott Peck, who has written about the importance of building true community, says the following in *A World Waiting to Be Born*:

> In his work on servant-leadership, Greenleaf posited that the world will be saved if it can develop just three truly well-managed, large institutions—one in the private sector, one in the public sector, and one in the nonprofit sector. He believed—and I know—that such excellence in management will be achieved through an organizational culture of civility routinely utilizing the mode of community.

4. *Service-Learning Programs*

A fourth application involves servant-leadership and experiential education. During the past twenty-five years experiential education programs of all sorts have sprung up in virtually every college and university—and, increasingly, in secondary schools. Experiential education, or "learning by doing," is now a part of most students' educational experience.

Around 1980, a number of educators began to write about the linkage between the servant-leader concept and experiential learning under a new term called *service-learning*. Service-learning has become a major focus for some experiential education programs in the past two decades.

The National Society for Experiential Education (NSEE) has service-learning as one of its major program areas. In 1990, NSEE published a massive three-volume work called *Combining Service and Learning*, which brought together many articles and papers about service-learning—several dozen of which discuss servant-leadership as the philosophical basis for experiential learning programs.

5. Leadership Education

A fifth application of servant-leadership concerns its use in both formal and informal education and training programs. This is taking place through leadership and management courses in colleges and universities, as well as through corporate training programs. A number of undergraduate and graduate courses on management and leadership incorporate servant-leadership within their course curricula. Several colleges and universities now offer specific courses on servant-leadership, including Gonzaga University in Spokane, Washington, where Shann Ferch and I teach several graduate courses in servant-leadership.

Since 2005, I have personally collaborated with Gonzaga University in the creation of the annual *International Journal on Servant-Leadership*, which is edited by Shann Ferch. Also, a number of noted leadership authors, including Peter Block, Ken Blanchard, Max DePree, and Peter Senge, have all acclaimed the servant-leader concept as an overarching framework that is compatible with, and enhancing of, other leadership and management models such as total quality management, systems thinking, and community-building.

In the area of corporate education and training programs, dozens of management and leadership consultants now utilize servant-leadership materials as part of their ongoing work with corporations such as Synovus Financial and Southwest Airlines. Through internal training and education, institutions are discovering that servant-leadership can truly improve how business is developed and conducted, while still successfully turning a profit.

6. *Personal Transformation*

A sixth application of servant-leadership involves its use in programs relating to personal growth and transformation. Servant-leadership operates at both the institutional and personal levels. For individuals it offers a means to personal growth—spiritually, professionally, emotionally, and intellectually. It has ties to the ideas of M. Scott Peck (*The Road Less Traveled*), Parker Palmer (*The Active Life*), and others who have written on expanding human potential. A particular strength of servant-leadership is that it encourages everyone to seek opportunities to both serve and lead others, thereby setting up the potential for raising the quality of life throughout society.

A Growing Movement

Servant-leadership works like the consensus building that the Japanese are famous for. Yes, it takes a while on the front end; everyone's view is solicited, though everyone also understands that his view may not ultimately prevail. But once the consensus is forged, watch out: With everybody on board, your so called implementation proceeds wham-bam.
—Walter Kiechel III, "The Leader as Servant," *Fortune* (May 4, 1992): 121–2.

Interest in the philosophy and practice of servant-leadership is now at an all-time high. Hundreds of articles on servant-leadership have appeared in various magazines, journals, and newspapers over the past decade. Many books on the general subject of leadership have been published that recommend servant-leadership as a more holistic way of being. In addition, there is a growing body of literature available on the understanding and practice of servant-leadership.

The Spears Center for Servant-Leadership (www.spearscenter .org) is an international, not-for-profit educational organization whose mission is to encourage the understanding and practice of servant-leadership around the world. Its programs include the creation of books, essays, journals, a newsletter, and other materials on servant-leadership, a partnership program, speaker services, and other elements. A series of servant-leadership anthologies (including this one) have included such noted leadership authors as James Autry, Peter Block, Max DePree, Stephen Covey, Margaret Wheatley, M. Scott Peck, and Peter Senge, to name but a few.

Life is full of curious and meaningful paradoxes. Servant-leadership is one such paradox that has slowly but surely gained hundreds of thousands of adherents over the past forty years. The seeds that have been planted have begun to sprout in many institutions, as well as in the hearts of many who long to improve the human condition. Servant-leadership is providing a framework from which many thousands of known and unknown individuals are helping to improve how we treat those who do the work within our many institutions. Servant-leadership truly offers hope and guidance for a new era in human development, and for the creation of better, more caring institutions.

In the end, it is the spirit of servant-leadership in individuals, in organizations, and in society, that offers one of the brightest hopes for the future of humanity.

Chapter One

SERVANT-LEADERSHIP AND THE INTERIOR OF THE LEADER: FACING VIOLENCE WITH COURAGE AND FORGIVENESS

Shann Ray Ferch

The light shines in the darkness, and the darkness cannot overcome the light.

—John 1:5

When night falls darkness comes, but at dawn, light illuminates the world. In the literature of humanity light is vision, clarity, and hope—the awaited answer to the cry heard in darkness. Servant-leadership is such a light: subtle, noted for its dignity, and shining on the edge of a broad landscape, drawing the people of the world to a fuller experience of what it means to be with one another. The human spirit, in its hope for interior depth, lasting community with others, and ascension toward the good, is the place from which all significant societal change emerges. Yet understanding of the human spirit remains elusive, a pearl of great price that is often out of reach and has become increasingly difficult to find in the attitudes, behaviors, and impacts that accompany the contemporary leader.

When a person is hidden, that person's leadership is also hidden, and he or she tends to use hidden measures such as dominance, manipulation, and fear. Such measures can be very effective, at times achieving powerful results, but they keep those who are led in darkness, subservient and oppressed. Servant-leaders become students of the areas of their own life they try to hide, working to bring these areas to light. They recognize the ways their leadership oppresses those they serve and seek to replace oppression with forgiveness, integrity, and reconciliation.

Robert Greenleaf, in his view of the interior of the person, returned the human spirit to a place of longing, an appropriate and refreshing longing that can result in a deep-seated sense of calling toward one another. From such a calling, the freedom to dream great dreams comes to the fore, as well as the will to see such dreams through to their completion. Until recently, it was difficult to envision anything but violence, atrocity, and death in war-torn Northern Ireland and apartheid-locked South Africa. Now, leaders such as David Hamilton in Ireland, and Nelson Mandela and Desmond Tutu in South Africa, have led the world to new ground, a ground fertile with the soil of forgiveness and tilled with a desire for truth, reconciliation, and restoration. In so doing they have pointed us to a more thoughtful sense of the interior of the leader in the midst of chaos and human evil. Such leaders are the modern-day expression of a long line of visionaries, leaders with foresight, able to hear the voice of others, and capable of leading in such a way that others are given greater life, greater light. In recent social history, Mohandas Gandhi and Martin Luther King, Jr., are the forerunners of today's leaders who live and work reflecting servant-leadership principles. Greenleaf's own words, elegant and discerning, are a clear statement of the interior richness and vision that accompany true leadership:

> I am hopeful for these times, despite the tension and conflict, because more natural servants are trying to see clearly the world as it is and are listening carefully to prophetic voices that are speaking *now*. They are challenging the pervasive injustice with greater force and they are taking sharper issue with the wide disparity between the quality of society they know is reasonable and possible with available resources, and, on the other hand, the

actual performance of the whole range of institutions that exist to serve society.

A fresh look is being taken at the issues of power and authority, and people are beginning to learn, however haltingly, to relate to one another in less coercive and more creatively supporting ways. A new moral principle is emerging which holds that the only authority deserving one's allegiance is that which is freely and knowingly granted by the led to the leader in response to, and in proportion to, the clearly evident servant stature of the leader. Those who choose to follow this principle will not casually accept the authority of existing institutions. *Rather, they will freely respond only to individuals who are chosen as leaders because they are proven and trusted as servants.* To the extent that this principle prevails in the future, the only truly viable institutions will be those that are predominantly servant-led.[1]

In an echo of Greenleaf's premise, the present viability of South Africa can be credited to the servant-leadership of people like Mandela and Tutu. By their exquisite personhood, they elicited the enduring love in the people of South Africa. Perhaps it was due to this vast love among Mandela, Tutu, and the people, that the people responded when these two leaders asked the country to respond in forgiveness, not with retribution, over the atrocities committed during apartheid. Mandela himself, upon his release after twenty-seven years of prison, forgave everyone from his jailers to the prosecutor who had unjustly imprisoned him.[2] Though South Africa, like any country, faces a difficult future, the response of the people, a response characterized by fullness, inimitable grace, and love, continues to revitalize the world political scene. South Africa remains one of the only governments in history to escape widespread political violence in the aftermath of a former violently oppressive regime.

Servant-leaders form the foundation of a free society, from the individual serving in the family community to the leaders of nations. In fact, it is especially those not in formal leadership positions that herald the coming of a more humane response to human evil. Such individuals are the bedrock of humanity, and in their presence we are given greater insight into others and ourselves. Because of their giftedness, the interior of the leader is no longer cloaked in hiddeness and fear, and we walk in a different light, the light of purpose and meaning.

Servant-Leadership and the Interior of the Leader

The discipline involved in growing the interior of the self creates a complex, often unwieldy, mystery for all who aspire to lead. Greenleaf's reversal of this aspiration forms a first step for many in the pursuit of a more compassionate and appropriately powerful interior. He stated that the true leader aspires first to serve and this simple revolutionary thought has unseated the entire historical foundation of most leadership traditions. The person who has lived and grown up under the command and control mentality finds it very difficult to turn the self toward servanthood. Even so, the underlying premise of servant-leadership becomes readily apparent whenever and wherever it appears. The essence of servant-leadership, shown in the subtle and graceful interactions between people, often takes us unaware, heals us, and draws us to a deeper sense of ourselves.

When I was a young boy, my mother's own manner of living was invaluable in helping me understand the interior of the servant-leader. A series of events occurred that would change the course of our family history. The following story reflects some of the uncertainties as well as the deep-seated desires that accompany family life, and that can become so crucial in later years when the opportunity to embrace servant-leadership presents itself more fully. Despite the initial intensity of the crucible that came to our family, a graceful outcome brought unforeseen nuances of hope.

I was nine years old. My brother, Kral, was eleven. We were in our parents' bedroom, a place we walked through quietly so as not to disturb anything. A mirror plate trimmed in silver lay flat on the

24

dark wood bureau, holding Mom's rings and lead crystal vials of perfume. We sat on the end of the bed, our feet hanging toward the floor. The bed was made military sharp, but the pillows were encased and tucked with a feminine hand. I think it was the femininity of it, and the absence of the masculine, that surprised and hushed us. Even then, I considered the great power Dad had over her. I think Kral and I felt deeply the facade of this room, the fear that held her here, her sanctuary in the evenings and into the night when he occupied the living room watching TV, or when his absence, when he was downtown drinking or whatever he did, became a silence in the home that was physical. I imagine her mind ran circles while she lay off to one side in the bed under the tight curve of clean sheets; she would have heard the sound of Kral and me breathing as we slept down the hall. At night we had heard her weep so many times it seemed uncountable.

We sat there, my older brother and I, in the elegant feel of that place, at the edge of the bed. We had never met in our mother and father's bedroom. We met here today. Our father had never cried in our presence. It would happen today.

My father is a big man, six foot four inches tall and weighing over 200 pounds. I remember how he held his hands together, and then pushed them against his forehead.

"Your mother and I are getting a divorce," he said.

He looked away. He pressed his hands together. He was standing above us.

"We can't seem to work it out. We're getting a divorce."

He stared at us and cried. "Well?" he said, still looking at us.

Mom looked to us also, into our faces. She was crying too.

Kral said nothing. I had no idea what Dad was saying.

"What does this mean?" I said finally. It was decades ago in Billings, Montana. I was in fourth grade, and at the time I didn't have a single friend whose parents were divorced. I don't think I understood the word.

"I'll be seeing you guys less," Dad said. "I'll be moving out."

I didn't say anything. Kral had his head down. Mom was quiet. The meeting ended.

This was the arrangement: Dad came home every other Tuesday night for an hour or two. On one such night when he was ten minutes in the door, my mom kicked him back out, cursing at him. I remember how his head and hands hung slack as he walked and how her fists pounded dents in his green down-filled jacket. She herded him over the front steps, along the front walk, and down the driveway. With our knees on the couch and our bodies leaned up the back of it, Kral and I watched from the front window, my arms folded tight over my chest. I touched my nose to the glass, and I saw Mom's face was red and heard her yelling at him.

"Stay away from my kids!" she said, and followed it with louder, sharper language. The words were hard, four-lettered words, ugly and new from her mouth, difficult to listen to.

Kral put his arm around me. He grabbed my hand and took me to the kitchen. Mom returned, gathered Kral and me in her arms in the kitchen, and sobbed. I had never heard my mother cuss, and she'd never been physical. She'd also never gotten her husband, directly, to do what she asked.

Dad continued to see us every other Tuesday night. Mom didn't attack him again. Dad took us to basketball games. He was a teacher and the head coach at Plenty Coups now, thiry-five miles south of Billings on the Crow reservation. He introduced Kral and me to his girlfriend. She was much younger than he. She worked with my father. The games were at the Shrine gymnasium, a small, hotbox in the middle of Billings, thick with the smell of people and popcorn and the blond lacquer of hardwood. The young athletes flew like birds. My father's boys—Marty Roundface and Max Spotted Bear, Tim Falls Down, and Dana Goes Ahead—often won.

At home, around the oval oak table in the kitchen, my mother sat with dead eyes, her hands folded in front of her.

"Is she prettier than me?" she asked.

Kral and I raced to answer first.

"No, Mom."

"Never."

"Not even close."

The darkness and the pain of this time was not the end of the story. Significantly, it actually turned into an astonishing new beginning. After a year of divorce, thanks to some very bold personal choices, they turned from their alienation and toward a meaningful understanding of God, and remarried. My mother had led the way, offering my father forgiveness for the grave wrongs he had done to her. Her courage opened the door for his new lifestyle, he overcame his alcoholism, decided to stop seeing other women, and returned to her, to the family. They formed a new marriage, thirty years strong now, and I have always been so proud of this accomplishment, so moved by their years of hard work. They remarried when I was ten years old, and I felt my mother was the cornerstone of their new way of life.

My mother grew up in Cohagen, Montana, a town of eight people. My father grew up in Circle, Montana, a town of 300. They remain in Montana, in Bozeman now, having moved first from Billings (where Dad coached the Crow players at Plenty Coups) to the Northern Cheyenne Reservation at St. Labre, from there to Livingston during my high school years, then on to Bozeman when my brother and I went to college. Some time back, on a visit to see them in Bozeman, I sat on the couch with my mother. Arched ceilings and oak beams lead to high, wide windows that look out on the Bridger Mountains and the Spanish Peaks, the view itself a reminder of the vast wilderness that is Montana and how thankful I am to have a good mother, a good father. We had grown up in trailers, three of them in three different towns. My parents had made sacrifices toward my brother's and my college educations, and I was happy for them, the life they had given us and the life they had built for themselves since then.

My mother was asking me about some of the research I was doing on forgiveness and touch, and I was telling her the stories of people—how they had hurt one another deeply, how they were seeking forgiveness and trying to return to the hope of a loving family. I thanked my mother for the forgiveness she gave my father. Even my choice of vocation as a systems psychologist and leadership consultant was in large part due to the integrity she brought to our family. Not surprisingly, that day as we sat on the couch, the natural, true way she carried herself shone through again.

After a pause in our conversation, she looked at me and said, "You know, I'd like to get together with you and ask your forgiveness for any of the harms I caused you growing up." She said the words with a pleasant look, a look of confidence and assurance. I have always loved that look, the way she carries herself with such strength even when dealing with things that are daunting, or cumbersome. She is a gracious person.

"That would be good," I said, "but I've harmed you as well. I'd like to ask your forgiveness too."

On my next visit to Montana, we ate dinner together at a quiet restaurant and had an evening of forgiveness-asking.

My father also taught me about the interior resilience of the servant-leader. Early on, my experience of him was often one of distance and anger. When it came to issues of leadership, command and control was the dominant style. In my recollection, he rarely expressed love verbally or physically. He often shamed my mother, and he lived a life that was self-possessed, wary of the influence of others, and highly defended. Then he changed. The first big change was his desire to return to the family after he and my mother divorced. This brave and beautiful choice on his part succeeded in reuniting our family and restoring much of our love for him. The second change came when my wife entered our family. She carried with her a vibrant, outgoing, and very expressive form of love. She said "I love you" often, she hugged everyone, she admitted her own faults, she was humble and open regarding the faults of others, and she drew out much of the love that was latent in my father. He gave himself to this influence and within a few years he had become more expressive, more verbally and physically loving, less rigid, and less distant. He became lovable; he had begun to love well.

I had come to town to go deer hunting with him. Deer hunting, in our family, has its own tension-filled history, so much that in our teens and early adulthood my brother and I refused to go hunting with our father, an avid outdoorsman. For me, hunting with my father coincided with loud tones, being dominated or discounted and made to go along with a relationship in which I felt demeaned. Now, because of my father's changes and the work we've done as a family, being outdoors together, hunting or fishing, is something we cherish.

When Jennifer and I come in the door after the seven-hour drive from Spokane, my father greets and hugs us. He kisses me on the cheek. He kisses Jennifer on the cheek.

"Good to see you," he says. "Glad you're safe."

He pulls us in, one at a time, to a full embrace. He is a big man with a bright smile. "I love you," he says.

That night he, Mom, Jennifer, and I eat together and talk. In the early morning, he sits on my bed and wakes me. "Time to get up," he says. His voice is gentle. He is happy we will be together today. He has prepared everything: boots, wool socks, wool pants, gloves, my coat, my hat, and our lunches. He prepares my breakfast and as we eat together, he reads something from the Bible, a line from Proverbs about how a friend loves at all times. He serves. We drive together in the early dark past the Bridger Range and through Livingston to a place outside Big Timber at the foot of the Crazy Mountains. He guides me as I shoulder the .243 Winchester, taking aim. He puts his hands gently on my arms, speaks softly as he shows me how to hold the rifle level. His voice reminds me to grow calm, to breathe deeply. In the silence of the valley, the shot rings out. He cleans and dresses the deer in an open field under a wide sky, and we work together in this, making things ready for the return home.

On the way back we stop to eat in a hamburger place in a small Montana town. As we enter the restaurant, he puts his arm around me and says, "You are a great son. Thanks for being such a great son." I am in my thirties, and still I want to cry. He speaks words most men don't speak. I am grateful he speaks them.

Shame and Forgiveness

Personal darkness and shame often accompany each other, and in darkness, vision becomes obscured. We have all experienced the shame of having wronged either ourselves or others, and the painful rift that results. For some of us the rift is momentary, or at least short-lived, but for others it develops into a chasm full of confusion and fear, something that seems uncrossable. The life that ends in work at the expense of intimacy...the life that ends in alcoholism, or cynicism, the hard despair that leads to suicide, the anger that creates a life of isolation and sorrow—people often live from shame and many die in it. Yet forgiveness, an element as vital as oxygen or water or fire, engenders a different, more profound experience of the world.

Every person has generated and sustained alienation in the self, the family, or the workplace. However, not all people have experienced the abiding loveliness of being welcomed back to community after having gravely wronged others. The servant-leader, familiar with the servanthood that develops life and mercy in others, is a person who seeks forgiveness for harming others and grants forgiveness to those who have done harm. Such forgiveness or compassion is given freely, not based on the willingness or remorse of the offender, but based on the higher vision of humanity to which the servant-leader is called. Forgiveness is not cheap; it requires a form of personal integrity that is hard-won. A certain lifestyle results, reflected in a humble awareness of one's own faults and the integration of strength, hope, and grace with regard to the faults of others. Forgiveness researcher Robert Enright, whose developmental stages help people develop forgiveness capacity, posits that the highest developmental level of forgiveness is forgiveness that is unconditional.[3] Preceding levels are often clouded by self-protection and the need for retribution while unconditional forgiveness is an overarching regard for the humanity evident even in the center of human evil. Greenleaf's call toward servanthood that creates wisdom and freedom, Martin Luther King's vision to love the oppressor, and Tutu's will to engender love through a forgiveness that heals our violence are potent expressions of the interior of the leader oriented toward healing the heart of the world.

Greenleaf, Martin Luther King, and Desmond Tutu lead us to greater light, greater clarity. The fine arts also provide a resonant voice for such illumination, for it is in honoring relationship and mystery that the arts undo the malaise that is too often evident in the family, the workplace, and the national psyche. There is a glorious light that makes darkness cower, and it is often found in works such as film, sculpture, and literature. In the following section, a story by Victor Hugo reveals the nature of leadership and the legitimate power and greatness that comprise the interior of the servant-leader.

Victor Hugo on Interior Wisdom and Freedom

Usually the leader who commands and controls has good intentions even while failing to see the impact of diminishment he or she is having on others. Attending to this impact, even giving others voice to articulate the ways they feel diminished in our presence and then making a meaningful response to their vision for us, can bring about more true relationships and organizations characterized by a sense of joy and liberty. But building the bridge from a character that is hidden or cloaked, self-consumed or self-absorbed, to one that leads through serving is often an arduous journey requiring consistent outside accountability and immense personal discipline. In the following paraphrase of a small portion of *Les Misérables*, Victor Hugo's priest reveals motives of goodness and hope and draws us to a better understanding of the interior of the servant-leader.

In the south of France in the late 1700s, there lived a condemned man, a man convicted when he was twenty-five for stealing a piece of bread to feed his starving sister. He was sentenced to five years in prison. Near the end of the fourth year, he escaped but was caught after two days and received three additional years for his attempt. In the sixth year he tried to escape, failed again, and was given five more years. The tenth year he tried and was caught again, and three more years were assigned. Finally, around the thirteenth year he escaped for four hours, was retaken, and three more years were tacked to his term, now nineteen years in all. At the end of his term he walked free, unable to find a single member of his family, determined to be incapable of loving, resigning himself to hatred and cynicism.

In those days, a criminal was required to identify himself to the magistrate immediately upon entering a town. Word then spread through the entire town almost immediately. After his release, the man enters his first town hoping to drink his first real drink, and sleep in his first warm bed in nearly twenty years. He reports his presence to the magistrate, then walks to the first pub, eager to spend a piece of the meager money he earned for his prison labor.

"Beer please," he says to the innkeeper, "I have money." And he places a coin on the bar in front of him.

The innkeeper smiles approvingly, "Beer it is then," he says and pours the prisoner a drink. Just then, a man approaches the innkeeper from the side and with cupped hand whispers in his ear. The innkeeper draws back the drink he has poured. He empties the glass back into the beer vat. "We don't serve your kind here," he says. "You'll have to go now."

The condemned man argues for himself, "I have money. I can pay."

"We don't serve your kind here," repeats the innkeeper.

"I can pay," says the condemned man.

"You will have to leave." The innkeeper does not change his stern face.

The condemned man leaves embittered and tries the tavern across the street, but here the host has already heard and the man is refused entry.

The man wanders the street in search of food and a bed. He sees the open glow of a window, a home, a family dining inside. He knocks at the door. He asks if he might sleep in the stable, perhaps share in the leftovers of their food. They push their children behind them. Their loathing is in their eyes, and with their voices, they despise him. They ask him to leave; they too have heard.

In the early dark of evening, he walks slowly and turns his face from all who pass him by. He finds a makeshift lean-to in the ill-kept garden of a small hovel. I will sleep with the dogs, he tells himself, and he moves on hands and knees into the warm, dark crawlspace of the hut. But he has invaded another's comfort; the sleeping dog awakens and bites his face. The man scrambles wildly back out into the street. I am even lower than a dog, he tells himself, and after walking at length, he sets himself down on the cobbled pavement to shut his eyes, to sleep on the stones beneath his feet.

He leans his head against a wall and closes his grimed face to wait for morning and to leave this place. But a woman's voice rouses him.

"Sir, can I help you?" She is a young nun and her face is kind.

"No," says the man. He looks angrily away from her.

"Will you sleep on the street tonight, friend?" she says.

"For nineteen years I've slept on a bed of wood, tonight it will be stone." He crosses his arms. He closes his eyes. "I am not welcome here."

"Have you knocked at every door?" said the woman.

"Yes."

"Have you knocked at that one?" the woman points.

"Which?" he asks.

"There," she says, "Knock there."

The man ignores her but after she has gone, he stirs himself and trudges to the door she mentioned. He knocks and is met by a priest. The priest welcomes him and prepares a table for him with bread, wine, and cheese. A bed is prepared as well. The man is dumbfounded. He sits and devours his food and he tells the priest, "I am a prisoner of nineteen years, a convicted thief, a condemned man."

The priest says, "This house is not mine, but Christ's. You are welcome here."

"I haven't hidden how despicable I am," says the man. "You don't even know my name. Yet you have treated me with kindness."

"Why would I have to know your name?" says the priest. "Besides, before you came, I knew it."

The man looks surprised, "You knew my name?"

"Yes," answers the priest. "Your name is my brother."

From the Interior of the Leader to Servant-Leading the World

Family systems writers such as Virginia Satir and Murray Bowen articulated the pain of families that promotes a sense of emptiness rather than wholeness. Their work leads to an understanding of the self not made of protectedness, privilege, or the abuse of power, but given, rather, to appropriate vulnerability, a sense of personal brokenness or humility, and the desire for mutual relationality that results in the legitimate power and greatness envisioned by Greenleaf. King and Tutu epitomize the central idea of servant-leadership on a social and global scale, having drawn the people of their country and the world to greater freedom, autonomy, health, and wisdom. Fittingly, both men also received the Nobel Prize for peace. The writings of Greenleaf, King, and Tutu provide a compelling spiritual vision of relationships meant for dignity, mutual respect, truth regarding personal failure, and the hope of a lasting reconciliation that can emerge from grave wounds to the self and the human community.

Greenleaf, King, and Tutu, leaders who have helped mend the human heart, are voices who condemn injustice and draw us to consider our own motivations and uses of power. In light of generational and historical processes of authority and submission, abuses of power result in the degradation of the weaker elements of any system, and inherently the more powerful elements as well. White colonialism and male authoritarianism are significant examples of this cycle, with people of color, women, and children suffering the results such abuses have generated, and whites and males often reflecting a coinciding poverty of spirit. Like many modern organizational leaders, today's fathers have often revoked their place of intimacy with beloved others, choosing a form of distance and isolation that is cloaked either in ambition or apathy. From the perspective of generational systems, those who grow up in an oppressive system tend to engender and live in oppressive systems throughout the lifespan and tend to evoke oppressive systems in the next generation. An amount of empathy is garnered for victim and victimizer from this perspective, as each person rises from a pattern of relationality that is continual and decidedly bound to humanity and the pain of the human condition. The abusive, depressed, or emotionally distant generational family; the organization that degrades people; the nation that is quick to war—these are all examples of how difficult it is to recognize and overcome our own considerable weaknesses, how difficult we find it to recognize and remove our own substantial lust to use coercion, force, or violence in the guise of leadership.

There is a need for change, not only internationally with regard to the atrocities of humanity, but here in our own cities. Races who have oppressed others can ask forgiveness of those they have oppressed: for the massacres and violence of the past, most often perpetrated by whites against people of color, against Native Americans, African-Americans, Asian-Americans, Hispanic Americans and others; and for the sense of entitlement and privilege that is often subtle and insidious today. Even now, our nation faces vast economic, political, and power-based distortion. A balance in these areas, rising from mutual endeavor, is one of the most pressing current avenues of servant-leadership. People in concerted action, seeking peace and greater relational—as well as economic—balance are leading the way. Recently at the site of the Big Hole massacre in Montana, where little more than a century ago Nez Perce women and children were massacred by U.S. cavalry, a ceremony of reconciliation took place, attended by descendents of both the Nez Perce and the U.S. cavalry members. Grace was extended and received, peace was given.

Other races, through openhearted living, are leading whites (generally of European descent) to a place of wholeness and restoration. Not surprisingly, such leadership finds its roots in the servant-first mentality. Larry Spears quoted Juana Bordas of the Center for Creative Leadership, who said

> Many women, minorities, and people of color have long traditions of servant-leadership in their cultures. Servant-leadership has very old roots in many of the indigenous cultures. Cultures that were holistic, cooperative, communal, intuitive, and spiritual. These cultures centered on being guardians of the future and respecting the ancestors who walked before.[4]

Similarly, people of poverty have the capacity to lead people of privilege to an idea of mutuality that can revolutionize the world poverty cycle and unseat the spiritual poverty that often afflicts the world's elite. Such a stance of life rising from death, though unfamiliar in circles of authoritarian power, has resonance in the natural world; it is the dawn of spring that follows winter's night, and each time we experience it we are thankful.

In present-day Montana, with its cold winters and far-distant towns, the love of basketball is a time-honored tradition. Native American teams, Cheyenne and Crow, Blackfoot and Sioux, have often dominated the basketball landscape, winning multiple state titles on the shoulders of modern-day warriors who are as highly skilled as they are intrepid. Basketball itself comes like a fresh new wind to change the climate of the reservation from downtrodden to celebrational. Plenty Coups with Mark Spotted Bear and Dana Goes Ahead won a couple of state championships in the early eighties. After that, Lodge Grass, under Elvis Old Bull, won three straight. Jonathan Takes Enemy is also counted among the most talented Native American hoop legends. He shot deep finger rolls with either hand, his jump shot was a thing of beauty, and with his quick vertical leap he could do a 360 dunk, with power. His senior year he averaged forty-one points per game in the state tournament. He and I had played basketball against each other numerous times in high school, our teams squaring off in notorious battles that are still mentioned by the old guard of hoop fans in the state. The competition was fiery and glorious, but then we went our separate ways. Recently we sat down again at a tournament in Billings. We didn't talk much about the past. He'd been off the Crow reservation for a number of years, living on the Yakima reservation in Washington now. He said he felt he had to leave in order to stay sober. He'd found a good job; his focus was on his family. The way his eyes lit up when he spoke of his daughter was a clear indication of the servant-leader, someone willing to sacrifice to enrich others. His face was full of promise and thinking of her, he smiled. She'll graduate from high school this year, he said, and it became apparent to me that the happiness he felt was greater than all the fame that came or the personal honors he had attained.

Bowen considered the true person as one capable of immense discipline in the center of human relationships, able to withstand his or her own desire to either attack or run, and instead to discern and maintain healthy relationship even in the face of power abuses.[5] Satir considered the true person a person of wholeness, wise, full, and congruent emotionally, physically, mentally, and spiritually.[6] This nexus of courageous living experienced by a person with strength of mind, heart, and spirit, is the kind of vision of leadership Greenleaf established in the workplace and King and Tutu established on the world political scene.

Regarding faith, Greenleaf, King, and Tutu lived and worked within a line of reasoning, emotion, and spirit that rose at least in part from their individual understanding of the Christian tradition. Significantly, it is important to note that much of the blood-spilling the world over for the last two millennia has been done in the name of Christianity, again indicating that threat and violence are too often a way of life, even for those seeking transcendence. While the ideas of Christ are important in the writings of Greenleaf, King, and Tutu, each man had deep-rooted respect for all people and found invasion of others in the name of religion, privilege, or any other source of power, repugnant. They embody a dignified respect for the human community in all its faith expressions. This balance of personal autonomy and connection to others is a vital aspect of their social leadership. Their approach articulates a just and lasting resolution of human pain, a resolution that leads through suffering, to a new, more whole sense of life. In their leadership, they cherished the lasting truths of every faith: respect for others, willingness to engage, and a sharp loathing for anything that degrades others.

A faith that violates others invalidates itself. Similarly, faith that subdues or suppresses itself often loses its vitality. Like all people, people of faith tend toward the extremes, either by trying to dominate others with their particular faith, or by silencing themselves in the attempt to do no harm. The balance of living one's faith while honoring others is accomplished beautifully by Greenleaf, King, and Tutu. Their work is both an expression of their faith in God, and their faith in people. I believe this comes from a personal, active understanding of love *and* power, the misuse as well as the potential of these, and the fulfillment that is the result of taking significant risks on behalf of the common good.

King and Tutu

King presented the timely notion that those who treat us poorly, harm us, or even seek to destroy us, are worthy of our own luxuriant and persevering love. To frame the person we disagree with in a dark light was to King a poison, something he intentionally fought against. King's work is prophetic and revolutionary and provides a look at the interior philosophy necessary for the growth of the servant-leader:

> Now I am aware of the fact that there are those who would contend that we live in the most ghastly period of human history. They would argue that the rhythmic beat of the deep rumblings of discontent from Asia, the uprisings in Africa, the nationalistic longings of Egypt, the roaring cannons from Hungary, and the racial tensions of America are all indicative of the deep and tragic midnight which encompasses our civilization. They would argue that we are retrogressing instead of progressing. But far from representing retrogression and tragic meaninglessness, the present tensions represent the necessary pains that accompany the birth of anything new. Long ago the Greek philosopher Heraclitus argued that justice emerges from the strife of opposites, and Hegel, in modern philosophy, preached a doctrine of growth through struggle. It is both historically and biologically true that there can be no birth and growth without birth and growing pains. Whenever there is the emergence of the new we confront the recalcitrance of the old. So the tensions which we witness in the world today are indicative of the fact that a new world order is being born and an old order is passing away.[7]

King's compelling vision for a future free of disharmony has provided clarity and light to people and nations the world over. He furthered the thought of the necessary growing pains involved in new life, a new life he called the new age, and he positioned forgiveness as one of its central callings.

A…challenge that stands before us is that of entering the new age with understanding and good will…virtues of love, mercy and forgiveness should stand at the center of our lives. There is the danger that those of us who have lived so long under the yoke of oppression, those of us who have been exploited and trampled over, those of us who have had to stand amid the tragic midnight of injustice and indignities will enter the new age with hate and bitterness. But if we retaliate with hate and bitterness, the new age will be nothing but a duplication of the old age. We must blot out the hate and injustice of the old age with the love and justice of the new.…Violence never solves problems.…

We have before us the glorious opportunity to inject a new dimension of love into the veins of our civilization. There is still a voice crying out in terms that echo across the generations, saying: Love your enemies, bless them that curse you, pray for them that despitefully use you.…

This love might well be the salvation of our civilization.[8]

For followers of King, even the most rabid racist is worthy of love, not because the racist deserves love, but because in loving, we see our own humanity in the humanity of the other and we are given strength to go forward and work to change destructiveness both in ourselves and in the systems around us. Tutu's discernment echoes that of King:

We are bound up in a delicate network of interdependence because, as we say in our African idiom, a person is a person through other persons. To dehumanize another inexorably means that one is dehumanized as well.[9]

…There is hope. There is hope because [we] are revealed as human beings, frail but with the capacity to do better if [we] get out of the self-justifying mode, the denial mode, and are able to say quietly, humbly, "I am sorry, forgive me/us."[10]

…I came away with a deep sense—indeed an exhilarating realization—that although there is undoubtedly much evil about, we human beings have a wonderful capacity for good. We can be very good. That is what fills me with hope for even the most intractable situations.[11]

...In relations between individuals, if you ask another person for forgiveness you may be spurned; the one you have injured may refuse to forgive you. The risk is even greater if you are the injured party, wanting to offer forgiveness. The culprit may be arrogant, obdurate, or blind; not ready or willing to apologize or to ask for forgiveness. He or she thus cannot appropriate the forgiveness that is offered. Such rejection can jeopardize the whole enterprise. Our leaders were ready in South Africa to say they were willing to walk the path of confession, forgiveness, and reconciliation with all the hazards that lay along the way. And it seems their gamble might be paying off, since our land has not been overwhelmed by the catastrophe that had seemed so inevitable.[12]

King and Tutu are excellent examples of the new critical depth being discovered in the discipline of leadership, a leadership that balances power, seeks to honor both masculine and feminine giftedness as well as a grand diversity of voices, and moves people toward greater richness with one another. Toni Morrison, a national treasure, turns a rapier-like wisdom toward understanding the human spirit. In her novel *The Bluest Eye*, she speaks of a young black girl who is plagued by the overwhelming opportunity given to those who have blue eyes (white girls). In a final statement, the black girl puts out her own eyes. The symbol of one person, plagued by another, one culture plagued by another—in which that other is at worst blatantly or violently authoritarian and at best oppressively indifferent—is the story of leadership superiority and entitlement throughout history. Significantly, Morrison's antihero, seeking the opportunity and privilege of her blue-eyed antagonists, loses her own vision in the process.

Under conditions that range from leader-ignorance to leader-dominance, a common component of the alienated relational environment is distorted vision. This cloudedness, or lack of clarity regarding hope, growth, and movement, takes on the quality of voluntary blindness in the immature leader. The leader grows defensive, resisting or even refusing growth. With an immovable, diseased heart, such a leader infects the family, the workplace, the culture, and society as a whole.

Three examples of a shift in the conception of the development and use of power are Burns' transformational leadership;[13] Komives, Lucas, and McMahon's relational leadership;[14] and Greenleaf's servant-leadership[15]—the last being the best expression of a transformational, relational leadership style. In these ways of thinking, harnessing power is something done not primarily for political or economic purposes, though these are natural ends of better leadership. Rather, the leader understands power and develops it for the good of self, family, and society. In the person able to be both a servant and a leader, love, with its dynamics of justice and mercy, is the most complete and appropriate form of power. The person who speaks love leads self and others well. The person who builds and furthers love is content.

Servant-leadership calls people toward a communal effort with others that both revitalizes the individual person and draws the community toward moral clarity; therefore, it requires a sustained effort at both personal and spiritual formation, the disciplined pursuit to understand the interior. This is the deepening and broadening of a person's character that results, without undo force, in the deepening and broadening of the character of others. Such a course of action is not done quickly because to serve others requires uncommon staying power, a vision not of minutes or days, but of years, decades.

In a poignant example of this, a woman once devoted herself to a calling that would serve society in the deepest way. Her calling was poetry and in the name of this calling, she forsook the typical trajectory of the modern life and devoted herself to the study of her art. She spent considerable time alone. She took menial jobs. For years, she read only the great poets. She listened to their rhythms, the elegance of their prose, and she tried in her own quiet place to write from the center of her heart. During this time, she rarely submitted her poetry to magazines, or literary journals, or publishers. She read, and she wrote, and at the end

41

of her long endurance, she released her poetry. For this poetry, for the patient music of her discipline and the bright understandings of her wisdom, in 1984 she was granted the Pulitzer Prize. Her name is Mary Oliver.

In one of her poems she captures a mystery. She wonders if at the end of life, instead of losing hope, we might still be like a bride wedded to amazement, like a bridegroom who gathers the whole world in his embrace. There is a long silence into which meaning emerges. When we live our lives in a rush, bound by a cacophony of sound, we lose hope.

Considering the time Oliver devoted to language, to the nuances of people and connection and to the hope of loving self and others and the world, her vision carries significant power. When we listen well, we recognize deeper meanings and become willing to grow and change. Oliver's vision echoes a similar movement in the relationships formed by the servant-leader: let us move toward an understanding of one another that leads us to know one another, to love one another. For the leader who is dominant, distant, or needy, and far from both the interior of the self and the interior of others, the lack of such love is a torment.

A person-to-person view of relating (Bowen[16]) infuses servant-leadership and becomes invaluable for people living and working in relational systems. A relational system is a community, be it a two-person community, a family-sized community, or larger communities such as business, work, and religion. Gardner, a leading leadership theorist, offers a list of necessary ingredients for community such as diversity, shared norms and values, free-flowing communication, an atmosphere of trust, effective participation in leadership, and an awareness of the larger systems to which the community belongs.[17] Komives, et al., furthered Gardner's work by defining community as the "binding together of diverse individuals committed to a just, common good through shared experiences in a spirit of caring and social responsibility."[18] Greenleaf's ideas focus leadership theory and practice to an even greater end—that of drawing the self and others toward greater personal health, wisdom, autonomy, and freedom. Such ideas bring about a new definition of work, relationships, marriage, fatherhood, motherhood, and family. The person who loves well finds the unique and gifted nature of his or her family members, coworkers, even those in authority, and then enhances this nature. The servant-leader does not detract from others. The servant-leader encourages, or "builds courage" in others. The development of community depends on leadership that values inclusion and strengthens all members to develop common purposes. Greenleaf, King, and Tutu provided servant-leadership in times when such leadership was a social necessity. The same necessity exists today.

Historically, leaders have tended to either attack when confronted by the relational environment, or run—both deeply destructive responses. On an individual level, leaders who honor relationships reverse this, fulfilling the more personal promise of Greenleaf, King, and Tutu's work. Rather than keeping people alienated or at a distance, such people draw us toward one another. They provide a cure for our hopelessness. They liberate us.

Early in our marriage, my wife asked me to help her make the bed. Another time she asked me to help her develop a presentation she would be giving at work. On a third occasion, she asked if I would like to go for a walk with her. My response to each of these requests was no. It wasn't that I wanted to say no; in fact I believe I wanted to say yes; it's just that there was always something else that took precedence, such as my need for rest, or my need to complete my own project instead of hers, or simply the undue importance I tended to place on my own agenda. It's not hard to see why my wife sometimes found me difficult to like. It was not until I grew more vulnerable, sacrificing my rigidity, that peace came to us.

Now consider the idea of people, leaders, who not only seek to say yes, but say yes and then follow through on the physical, emotional, and spiritual requests of their loved ones. They will be honored by their loved ones; their loved ones will speak well of them and desire to be near them. So too in the workplace. I have been a part of a group of men who have met weekly for the last fourteen years, good men devoted to the beloved people of their lives. Through the influence of these men, I am learning to say yes to the promise of intimacy in self, family, and work, and to realign myself from being a man of distance and defensiveness, to becoming a man of listening, responsiveness, and tenderness.

The Love that Heals Society

In any system in which power is used willfully toward self-advancement at the expense of others, oppression and injustice tend to take root. King and Tutu do not commend a placating or passive response to such injustice, but rather a form of "nonviolent militancy" that actively pursues the restoration of the human community. This view of human nature recognizes the propensity for violence—against self and others, physically, sexually, emotionally, intellectually, culturally, spiritually—in every person. People who actively uncover their own ways of oppressing others become leaders who seek and form relationships of mutual respect with others, with authority figures, women and men, and with their own children. The development of spirituality, free of the diminishment of self or others, is the hope of the servant-leader. People of maturity can live from a sense of creative wholeness in light of faith, and the difference in their character is a notable difference; their countenance, their personhood, is as strong as it is loving and kind. Such people are powerful and gentle and ultimately they live a more true, more fulfilling life. For the leader who is distant and isolated, fortified and remote, a return to a real self and to the welcoming embrace of loved ones is deeply refreshing. This person, the mature person who loves well and is well loved, becomes the natural servant and leader of others.

Greenleaf echoes history's clarion call for a justice that restores us to one another through acceptance, forgiveness, and love. "We have known this for a long time in the family. For a family to be a family, no one can ever be rejected."[19] He opens a view of love that is personally and collectively responsible, not only for our wrongs but also for the greatness of our dreams. "Love is an indefinable term, and its manifestations are both subtle and infinite. But it begins, I believe, with one absolute condition: unlimited liability! As soon as one's liability for another is qualified *to any degree*, love is diminished by that much."[20]

In the crucible of people, faith, and work there are many

dualities and hypocrisies. These can also become the lived experiences that invite us past simple answers to the reflection and contemplation involved in forming a lasting sense of existence. We often reveal our national tendency to condemn, criticize, and diminish others rather than striving to articulate our own emptiness, our own abiding sense of personal weakness, or our need for help and wholeness. King David of Hebrew lore, one of the most beloved of all the kings of history, was said to be the friend of God. He was considered a man after God's own heart. This seems to be an ugly irony, considering that in scripture, David is also shown to be an abuser of power, a murderer, and an adulterer. Such a desperate paradox, though extreme, is not unfamiliar to the lives of most leaders.

David had become complacent; he was letting others fight battles he should have fought. One day, while looking down from the high place of his castle he saw a woman bathing. Her name was Bathsheba. He found her beautiful, and he was struck by the sudden desire to have her. In his passion, David impregnated Bathsheba. Upon discovering that she was married to Uriah, one of David's most loyal and skilled soldiers, David became distressed. Through a devious succession of events, he succeeded in having Uriah killed on the front lines by withdrawing Uriah's surrounding warriors in the heat of a bloody conflict. David proceeded to hide what he'd done, acting as if the balance of his kingship, morality, and relationality remained noble. The lifestyle he exemplified at this time—a lifestyle of dominance, sexual greed, the abuse of power, and pervasive hiddenness—is the lifestyle of leaders locked in the command and control mentality. In a turn of grace, but not without terrible cost, David moved from command and control to personal brokenness, willingness to hear of the great wrongs he had done, willingness to try to make amends, and a desire to move with renewed integrity and care for the human community. It was in the perseverance and eventuality of this turn that he was brought again to a place of respect.

Like David, and like others who aspire to lead, we are people, and therefore fallible and beautiful at the same time. It is in facing the dark tragedies of life, facing death or the threat of death in the self, in others, and in the community that we are given opportunity to create a vessel that is profound, and worthy. Greenleaf's insight gives hope:

> To be on with the journey one must have an attitude toward loss and being lost, a view of oneself in which powerful symbols like *burned, dissolved, broken off*—however painful their impact is seen to be—do not appear as senseless or destructive. Rather, the losses they suggest are seen as opening the way for new creative acts, for the receiving of priceless gifts. Loss, *every loss one's mind can conceive of*, creates a vacuum into which will come (if allowed) something new and fresh and beautiful, something unforeseen—the greatest of these is *love*. The source of this attitude toward loss and being lost is *faith*: faith in the validity of one's own inward experience; faith in the wisdom of one's history, events in which one's potential for nobility has been tested and refined; faith in doubt, in inquiry, and in the rebirth of wisdom; faith in the possibility of achieving a measure of sainthood on this earth from which flow concerns and responsibility and a sense of rightness in all things. By these means mortals are raised above the possibility of hurt. They will suffer, but they will not be hurt because each loss grants them the opportunity to be greater than before. Loss, by itself, is not tragic. What *is* tragic is the failure to grasp the opportunity which loss presents.[21]

In a fitting tribute to making meaning of tragedy, many of the people of South Africa have not only forgiven the offending party, but also invited the offender back to the center of the community, calling each other brother and loved one, sister and friend. Ramsey's[22] breakthrough research on South African perpetrators of violence and their experience of being forgiven and reconciled with the victim's family shows that it is not strong-armed justice that brings us closer to the better angels of our nature, but mercy...and from this mercy, true justice emerges. Her most important finding was that it is not the repentance of the perpetrator that builds the necessary bridge, but the unconditional forgiveness of those who were harmed. Amy Biehl was stabbed multiple times and killed by a militant black mob during apartheid. The mob did not know she was a young Fulbright scholar at the time, working to topple apartheid. Ramsey interviewed her parents, who remained in South Africa and offered forgiveness to the violent offenders. Ramsey's work reveals that in each case of forgiveness it was an unrelenting love that overcame the stolid denial and even haughtiness shown by the offenders. Today, the men who killed Amy Biehl call Amy's mother their mother, and she calls them her sons; a complete reversal and unraveling of hatred, and the weaving of a new tapestry of love.

In another of Ramsey's cases, a white member of the apartheid security police conducted a night attack on what he believed to be a black arms house. He was mistaken and eleven innocent people were killed, among them women and children. After the Truth and Reconciliation Commission hearings, he went to the village to admit to his wrong and seek forgiveness. The people refused and banished him. Amazingly, in a turn of grace two years later, the people brought him back for a day of reconciliation in which the families of the victims offered him forgiveness and invited him to live in the village. He was dead until that day, he said. After that day he lived. Now he works raising funds to construct a community center, hand-in-hand with those whose family members he killed.

Another white woman whose daughter was killed in a black militant action offered forgiveness and reconciliation to the man who commanded her daughter's death. In a cultural ceremony in the man's home village, special names were given to her and to him. The names symbolize a unique greeting so that each time the two meet they can greet one another in this way. In translation, one asks of the other, "Where are you?"—the response is, "I am with you." Today they speak together internationally in honor of forgiveness.

Such stories of indelible courage give credence to one of the most intriguing hopes of humanity, that in the depths of our interior not only do we find the capacity for violence, but more importantly, we find the subtle and steadfast presence of overwhelming grace. Grace. This complex, often mysterious way of being—God-given, I believe—is capable of moving us from a position of the need for justice to a position that doesn't silence or forget about or forgo justice. Rather, it holds faithfully to justice but with a heart of tenderness, mercy, and love toward humanity—all of humanity, including the most evil among us; and in fact identifies the evil not as individual and separate from the self, but as a part of our own individual and collective humanity in need of healing, dignity, and restoration.

Conclusion

The interior balance between darkness and light, an honest accounting of our own darkness, and the choice to approach and humbly seek light may be the most durable metaphor of relational intimacy. Leaders who give themselves over to the most hope-filled wishes of the human community, the most important of our dreams, become the servant-leaders who walk in such a way that others become wise, healthy, and free.

In our own country, the bloodline of violence runs deep. The poverty of our age is the exaltation of the self, the objectification of the other as a product to be used, a consumable to be consumed—too often a philosophy of self-gratification supersedes the consideration of the other as beloved, as sacred. It is in this poverty of mind that we first commence to do violence to one another. Consider the rate of sexual addiction in our society, the violence in our schools, and the emotional and intellectual violence associated with our organizational and political culture. Violence in its most insidious forms shrouds the interior of our nation. The servant-leader, devoted to the moral and loving depths of the interior, becomes a light to the generations, bringing hope and direction amid the confusion. It is in the heart of forgiveness that the heart of violence is brought to its appointed place, a place of mercy and restoration. My eldest daughter Natalya, seven years old, came to me recently and sat on my lap while I was typing at the computer.

"Can I write a story?" she said. "You type it in, Daddy."

"Sure," I said, and holding her, I typed the words. This is what she said:

And sparkles came out of her eyes. And then she looked out the window and darkness clouds came out of the sky and then the next morning the sun came out and she was surprised, and she glimmered in beauty and long hair, she became the beautifullest, prettiest girl in town.

The vision I have for my daughters is that theirs is a beauty not merely physical, but a beauty of the heart, the mind, and the spirit. In this vision, I hope in the inimitable voice of Martin Luther King who said: "Everybody can be great, because everybody can serve…you only need a heart full of grace, a soul generated by love."[23] Grave human evil is a darkness that has accompanied humanity from the beginning of time, yet light in its ultimate transcendence cannot be subdued and when it comes, it fulfills its purpose, taking away our fear, leading us to the dignity of humanity, giving us a new vision, surprising us. I believe it is due to the heroic resilience of the human spirit, the bright interior of the servant-leader, that the words of the Lebanese poet Kahlil Gibran still ring so true:

"The strong of soul forgive."[24]

Chapter Two
CÉSAR E. CHÁVEZ: SERVANT-LEADERSHIP IN ACTION

María D. Ortíz

A Personal Perspective

Why is it important to study the life and work of César E. Chávez? Growing up in my grandmother's household in Veracruz, Mexico, in the early 1950s, I often listened to her praying that her sons, my father and uncles, would never go north as *braceros*. I did not quite understand why she would pray so vehemently with the same plea every evening. Later on, in 1970, when I arrived in the United States and began attending college, I often heard about the grape boycotts, the Chicano Movement, and César Chávez, all in one sentence, or within one mixture of emotion and rhetoric that was either approving or disapproving. The emotional overtones often were disapproving, as the political-cultural context of my environment in a small college town in Utah was intolerant of "revolutionary" and "resisting" attitudes, and the struggles of the Civil Rights Movement in the early 1970s. Soon it began to dawn on me that my grandmother's prayer on behalf of my father and uncles must have had something to do with the social struggle of the agricultural workers or *mojados*, as my sociology teacher used to call them in Sociology 111 (The Study of Social Conflicts).

This sociology professor, a Mexican immigrant himself, would lecture us (mostly international students) about the necessity of leaving behind old traditions and adopting new ways of thinking that reflected "appropriate" American cultural values, because these would lead us into a successful life of accomplishment and happiness. Then he would illustrate our fate if we did not do so, with case samples from the current headlines on the "social problems" caused by nonconformist social minorities. It seemed odd to me he would say that. My experience and sense of personal history strongly told me that abandoning one's traditions, memories, and history was not even possible without inflicting harm to the psyche. I knew that my having been born and raised in Mexico was an undeniable, indelible truth that would be with me for the rest of my life. It was my personal history. My grandmother's prayer gained more significance.

Those days were fun, exciting, and hard-working days for me; I am glad I did not pay much attention to my sociology professor. Our social group of international students provided much support and nurturing. My work in the Latin American Student Association, and my participation in religious community activities with other Latin American students, was an education in itself. The 1970s were years of much political turmoil in various Latin American countries: Chile, Argentina, Peru, and Bolivia all saw their share of military takeovers that involved obvious U.S. intervention. These were also countries of origin for many of my fellow students. My roommates, several from Argentina and Chile, would bring us together every weekend. Sitting in circles on the floor of our small basement apartment, we would spend hours discussing U.S. international policy and its impact on our families back home. We argued about the abundance of paradox we witnessed every day, and we hungered for justice, peace, and acceptance in an environment where we could not show our discontent or "true" self without consequence to our immigration status. Often we would end those nights dancing and singing with renewed enthusiasm for the week ahead of us. I lost many dear friends after they quietly decided to leave school, or the country all together, because their personal struggles in dealing with the many contradictions in our lives became unbearable.

I went on to study organizational behavior in graduate school and then to doctoral work in systems theory and phenomenology as a method of inquiry. My intellectual pursuits provided me with a conceptual "handle" to juggle the contradictions I discovered during my college years. I had the opportunity to test several theories learned in my studies by applying them to my work as public policy advisor on Hispanic issues to Utah governor Norm H. Bangerter in the late 1980s.

Then, as director of the Hispanic Advisory Council for Utah, I confronted the movement to make English the official language of the state. I saw the passion of the Hispanics in Utah to defend their right to speak the language of their heritage, and the many allies they had, who also defended that right. My job with the Hispanic Council allowed me to have the governor's ear and to communicate the desires of the Hispanic community against pending legislation that would make English Utah's official language. The legislation was symbolic and offensive to a minority population that still felt left out by a cultural and religious majority in a state where 70 percent of the population belongs to the religious tradition of the state's founders. This majority has significant political influence on many of the state's institutions. The Church of Jesus Christ of Latter-day Saints (commonly referred to as the Mormons) purportedly has a long tradition of language training and cultural outreach in its worldwide missionary efforts. At any given time, about 60 percent of all Mormon households have sons and daughters in a foreign mission or at the missionary training center learning a second language. At the same time, this collective social and cultural experience in foreign countries, dependent on the goodwill of many, often builds great tolerance and acceptance for cultural and linguistic diversity. Once again, the emerging paradoxes were fascinating and challenging.

Leaving Utah for a job in Washington, DC, allowed me to sort through various personal experiences. I had been consistently puzzled at the meaning of all these experiences and their implications in my work with organizations. I left Utah with an interesting perspective on the challenges of creating and maintaining community while affirming my personal identity and history.

I began my academic career in 1991 after completing my doctoral work and relocating to the heart of Silicon Valley. Soon, I found myself teaching in a Mexican American studies program in the California State University system. There I endeavored to merge my academic training in organization theory and my professional experience in public policy with the demands of an established curriculum that required integration of historical, cultural, and political content.

It seemed that the social label "Hispanic," as a racial or ethnic identifier, no longer applied in this new, politically defined organizational context. It also did not apply to the demographic population that the Census Bureau labels "Hispanic," an acceptable term in some Midwestern states and on the East Coast. However, in California my students would sometimes challenge me if I failed to use *Chicano* or *Chicana* when referring to the same demographic segment labeled "Hispanic" in the U.S. Census. Obviously, the meanings attached to these labels have more to do with the local politics and geographic location than they do with truth and the integral identity of the bearer of the label.

The dynamics of this experience urged me to develop and write a teaching strategy with segments of class activity and discussion on social construction, and the social functions of ethnic and racial labels. I learned about various pedagogies, such as collaborative learning, group projects, and interactive work using electronic multimedia. Here my training in organization theory and systems thinking came in very handy and it allowed me to navigate the "emotional undercurrents"[1] of a multicultural classroom with some ease. My learning and growth as an educator were satisfying. Yet my department chair was unhappy and uncertain of my true "identity," for he would often mumble, "But are you really a Chicana?" And Chicano activist students sitting in my classes for the first time would also challenge my identity as a Chicana by often asking "but what are you?" to which I would answer, "It depends on what you mean by the label Chicana." My experience emerging from these questions of identity clearly illustrated the impact of misconceived and misperceived identity on relationships. I saw how information could be manipulated for the benefit of individuals controlling meaning in politically defined organizational contexts.

These various experiences concerning identity and community have kept me intimately connected to the question of how we create living systems that sustain all of our differences and similarities. How do we create living systems where the strength and well-being of those systems is measured by the strength and well-being of each one of its individual members?

A Problem of Meaning and Identity in Politically Defined Systems

In politically defined systems, I have experienced the contextual nature of our lives as an intricate woven design constructed upon various layers of meaning. As individuals, we develop personal identities anchored on sets of values, beliefs, traditions, and attitudes. From the perspective embedded in our personal lives, we create interpersonal systems and we enter into relationships. We create families. We organize into communities. We join associations and clubs. All these become our groups of reference. The dynamics of our interpersonal relationships, whether they serve us well or not, guide us as we encounter additional layers of meaning embedded in our social institutions and society. Often, the fundamental meaning of our personal lives does not harmonize with the ethos and the various meanings ascribed to us by these politically defined systems.

Frequently in these organizational settings, the discrepancies between our personal context of meaning and the messages from a politically defined system can be loud and incompatible with the essence of our values, beliefs, traditions, or desires. For example, the meaning of the labels given to us by society based on our place of birth, biological makeup, spiritual or religious choices, and different levels of income, often do not match the meaning of who we believe we are, or what we can be. We know on a collective-instinctual level that institutional or societal labels do not establish the truth about our personal selves. Yet, not a single life can be fully experienced, for we always seem to operate from the disadvantage of intricate designs of meaning that can be manipulated at will. The societal messages in politically defined organizational contexts contain bits of meaning but they are lacking in "truth." At best, we can strive to interpret those bits of meaning and articulate our interpretation of the world by establishing our "truth" with our actions.

There Is an Opportunity for Learning and Finding Solutions

The immigrant experience presents an opportunity to learn about self-organizing systems and the nature of servant-leadership within these contexts. In learning about the process of self-organizing and servant-leadership we need to shed the lenses prescribed by disciplinary academic training, and rely more on various ways of viewing reality and truth. An interdisciplinary approach is always useful. The social sciences and the humanities offer various tools to help us organize and communicate a rich array of experiences. The study of social movements often occupies great attention of our politicians and sociologists, yet much meaning and effort is lost because we often limit the incorporation of the other aspects in social movements that historically were responding to real human need and sorrow. How can we begin learning about these movements and their self-organizing nature? And how do we engage in the ongoing dynamic of self-organizing living systems to change the context of politically defined systems that do not serve us well?

Studying the life of César Chávez and the specifics of his work with the farmworkers has helped me recover what I did not learn in Sociology 111 in the early 1970s, and satisfy some of that hunger for a better world—a world that still seems so distant, one that I learned to dream of with my fellow Latino students in Provo, Utah. I will highlight the connection of the work of César Chávez with the concept of the servant-leader; this concept suggests an important gateway to creating a better society. My perspective is of one identified as Mexican born, an immigrant, a single woman, a non-Catholic, and a naturalized American citizen who was "privileged" to receive a postgraduate education in private American institutions. The burden of the meaning ascribed to these social labels in the aggregate can make my task of articulating this connection difficult at one level, yet easy at another. What it guides me to is the insight gained in my personal struggle to search and define "my" essential truths; and a desire to assert my conviction in the transcending nature of one man's life and work. For in doing so I am also asserting my personal history and experience.

César Chávez: The Man and the Servant-Leader

> One saw in him what one wanted to see. For religious clergy it was a Christian movement; for youth, it was a communal-mystical movement; for political radicals, it was a labor-class struggle; for liberal intellectuals and politicians, it was a movement of hope and the American essence; and for others, Chávez was another Gandhi.[2]

In looking for a way to write about César Chávez, there is one salient question: What is the essence of this man? There is no consensus on the answer to that question. Some, including Andrés Irlando, have questioned whether there needs to be a consensus. "We make our heroes," says Irlando, "and we need to remember that in our biases we tend to go one way or the other. The legacy speaks for itself."[3]

César Chávez triumphed as a leader among those who followed him because he knew how to be a servant first. I highlight the connection between César Chávez's life work and the concept of the servant-leader. In doing so, I draw directly on the recollections of those whose lives were shaped by his service and leadership. These recollections come mainly from interviews recently conducted among people who were active in the farmworker movement in Santa Maria Valley and Guadalupe, California. They represent a microcosm of people that made the movement possible in the Santa Maria Valley. They are a representative sample of the many people that were involved across the country in their own communities.[4]

The imprint of this record underscores a passion for service and action. His leadership had a purpose, to serve and create a community of service that would enhance the servant's life among other things.

The Servant-Leader

> Part of the human dilemma is that the meaning of *serve*, in practical behavioral terms for both persons and institutions, is never completely clear. Thus, one who would be servant is a life-long seeker, groping for light but never finding ultimate clarity. One constantly probes and listens, both to the prompting from one's own inner resources and to the communications of those who are also seeking. Then one cautiously experiments, questions, and listens again. Thus the servant-seeker is constantly growing in self-assurance through experience, but never having the solace of certainty.[5]

Robert K. Greenleaf introduced the concept of the servant-leader in a 1970 essay *The Servant as Leader*.[6] Greenleaf elaborated this concept within the context of management practice in business organizations, and his ideas exerted an influence on leadership training and management development programs throughout the 1970s and 1980s. In the 1990s, after Greenleaf died, his philosophy evolved to become the mission statement of the Greenleaf Center: "To fundamentally improve the caring and quality of all institutions through a new approach to leadership, structure, and decision making." It incorporates three goals: to increase service to others; to take a holistic approach to work; and to promote a sense of community among workers and the sharing of power in decision making.

In recent years, the servant-leader concept has been applied to the practice of service-learning in community service on college campuses; work among youth, and some ecumenical programs. This essay will draw from the concept of the servant-leader as developed by Robert K. Greenleaf.

In his narrative of how he thought of the term, *servant-leadership*, Greenleaf recalls reading *The Journey to the East* by Hermann Hesse. In it, Leo, the servant of a group of men on a mythical journey, is the central figure, performing menial tasks while sustaining the group with his spiritual presence. Greenleaf's interpretation leads to the conclusion that a great leader is a servant first.

> The servant-leader is servant first....It begins with the natural feeling that one wants to serve, to serve first. Then conscious choice brings one to aspire to lead. He or she is sharply different from the person who is leader first, perhaps because of the need to assuage an unusual power drive or to acquire material possessions. For such it will be a later choice to serve—after leadership is established.[7]

How Was Chávez a Servant?

I draw upon the words of some of those who knew Chávez well and remember him. Paulino Pacheco, one who knew Chávez since 1969, remembers him this way:

> He came from a peasant family. His grandfather was a peasant; he came from Mexico when he was two years old. His father was also a peasant. So he knew the life of a peasant. He knew what it is like. He knew the suffering and enslavement of peasantry. When we were struggling, his message was "We fight together. We fight for a cause and we do not use violence." And so we stay together and fight for our cause, for our race, and for our rights. We stick together for justice.[8]

César Chávez began his work in his childhood, with the people he encountered as he toiled side-by-side with them in the fields of California. He knew from personal experience what it meant to be a servant, and what a servant does for those he would serve. More importantly, he knew what material things he did not need in order to lead a decent life serving others. When Alfred Athie, one of César's bodyguards, was asked if he thought César had a lot of power, he answered:

I don't think it was power. He didn't like power. I don't think he ever used power. For that reason, we sought him. He searched for something that occupied him. What we felt, all the people felt…helping people, seeking justice.…He never looked for anything for himself. He could see he had been a part of this class of people. He had grown up in the fields; and how many things and how many prohibitions had been in the life of his parents, his brothers and family. I think this is what made him see, with compassion, the necessities. He wasn't searching for power, but for solutions; seeking a way of living with people, with the worker, with the owners of the lands.[9]

He devoted his life to carving out justice for farmworkers out of long grueling negotiations with growers, and to alerting the public and anyone who would listen to the dangers of pesticides. He, along with Dolores Huerta, spoke early and without compromise about the dangers of pesticides in the fields and in our food.[10] Indeed, "Because toxic-pesticide use has always been a major concern of Chávez, the union's first contracts with Delano area table-grape growers contained strong pesticide protections for farm workers, including a prohibition on the use of DDT, Aldrin, Dieldrin, and Parathion on union ranches."[11]

The personal was unavoidably political, and in this context, this man was human at his best. When it was necessary for him to have personal protection due to serious threats to his life, he did so in ways that would prevent violence by requesting that no guns would be carried by his bodyguard.[12] When negotiating with unsavory characters, he found it almost incomprehensible how difficult some of them could be.[13]

He was imperfect. In his imperfection, he was capable of making mistakes and learning from them. At the same time, he saw the need to change, as the UFW demanded of him as a manager facing the evolution of a growing organization. "In his words: 'The world was really changing. Now we had to start planning. We had to talk about restructuring the union. We had to look at what we were doing.'"[14] The persistent message from those who worked with him is one of service. Service done mostly by example, serving those (the volunteers that became organizers and union leaders) that would be "servants" to others.

> And when I say, strive to help people, he educated us in the sense that you don't do it for profit, you don't do it for self gain, you do it because there's a need to do it. And people need to have somebody there to help them…you know "walk that walk." He never got money, he never got riches or anything like that, and most of us do the same thing now, following through with his legacy—doing what he did, without pay. I do it today.[15]

César Chávez also mediated between the opposing currents of peaceful demonstrations, and the steadfast social struggle required to overcome political and economic injustice. He studied eastern philosophies, read about Gandhi and his accomplishments in India, and learned about economics, political strategies, and management. Without his direct experience in the fields as a servant to others, he could not have understood the practical implications of leading others in the creation of social change. Near the end of his life, he still faced the uncertainties of political unresponsiveness and injustice.

How Was César Chávez a Leader?

Robert Greenleaf stated, "Leadership was bestowed on a man who was by nature a servant. It was something given, or assumed, that could be taken away. His servant nature was the real man, not bestowed, not assumed, and not to be taken away. He was a servant first."[16]

In brief, I will focus on two areas in connection with the main concept of the servant-leader as developed by Robert Greenleaf, and later advanced by Ken Blanchard, Larry Spears, Peter Block, and Margaret Wheatley. Blanchard proposed two important aspects of leadership that have been widely discussed in the relevant literature: the "visionary" part, and the "implementation" part.[17] The first aspect has to do with determining what to do in a given situation—that is "doing the right thing." The second concerns "doing things right," or the implementation of the task of leadership. These two elements are not mutually exclusive, and the success of leaders depends on their capacity to understand their interconnectedness within the social systems of the followers.

Now, if we look at these two aspects in the context of César Chávez's life work, it seems that he knew well what the right thing was and how to do it, even in the most unusual circumstances. The following passage illustrates how he responded to complex situations that were abundant in tragedy and complicated by political struggle:

I called César and told him one of our members had died. César asked how old he was, because the death benefit depended upon his age. I told him he was 30-years-old. César said his benefit would be $1000. César asked where his family lived and I told him he had only his mother. César said to bring his mother and we would have a fiesta to raise money to help her out with the funeral expenses. César said to call the newspapers, make up a HUGE check, and hold it up in front of the television. We had the fiesta and gave his mother the check so she could return home. We had a lawyer there to make sure it was all in proper order. It was all taken care of. Two weeks later, he called me and asked how things were going. I told him that there was a long line of people waiting to join and César said, didn't I tell you that there would be a miracle. People were joining the union.[18]

This passage illustrates how Chávez recognized three clear imperatives in the situation before him and how each imperative required a different, yet appropriate response. First, at the personal and interpersonal levels, there was tragedy, sorrow, and financial hardship. Second, the entire farmworkers' union community had to come together to strengthen each other in cooperation and celebration. And third, on the political-societal level, it was necessary to advance the goal of increasing the union's membership by asserting the benefits of this organization to those that would join them. His action contained a response that addresses each one of these imperatives. The deceased was a single young man killed in a car accident. He was a farmworker and member of the union, at a location where efforts to gain new members had been exhausting. The local union organizer and recruiter was demoralized and in need of direction. César's response acknowledged the interconnectedness between the individual and the institution that can help him; in this case, the union. He then provided the direction for specific appropriate action. His response was consistent with the aspect of leadership discussed by Blanchard—the visionary part of knowing *what to do*, and second, the implementation part of *doing it right*.

Leadership was bestowed upon him by those he sought to serve, according to farmworker Maria Baca:

> We are trying to teach our children and grandchildren that this man was a leader. He will continue to be a leader even after he is gone. His name will continue to be a leader. No one else will be put in his place, because that is what he was. César was a leader. He was for education and for the poor. He would suffer. I saw that man cry when he could not help these people. I saw everything. I had compassion for that man, because he was not doing it for himself, he was doing it for his people. For the children of today and tomorrow and the years to come; that was his purpose.[19]

Greenleaf writes that the "best test and the most difficult to administer" rests on a few simple but hard questions: "Do those served grow as persons? Do they, while being served, become healthier, wiser, freer, more autonomous, more likely themselves to become servants? And what is the effect on the least privileged in society; will they benefit, or, at least, not be further deprived?"[20]

These questions are asked of managers and leaders within the context of business organizations and multinational corporations where success is measured, in many instances, by the amount of quarterly profits. These questions are significant, whether they are applied directly in the context of the business world or they are applied as a test of the servant-leader notion as exhibited by the work of César Chávez. Once again, the answer comes from the memories of those he sought to serve.

> So, we went to a meeting in Santa Maria and César was there. He said, "Don't worry, I'll get you a lawyer, but you have to fight for an education for your children. Fight now!" When he said "Fight now" it was so important for us. We had never done that, our parents had never fought for us and it was important for us to fight for our children. We are still fighting for a better education for our children. I have grandchildren now—tomorrow I might have great-grandchildren—and I want it to be better for them. I want something better. César gave us that....Thank God, he gave us that! He gave us a good education. The whole thing was, not only to be a farm worker, but also to get a good education. He brought us that education, and what we are learning now.[21]

Because of the experiences many farmworkers gained as organizers and members of the UFW, their children were influenced to see beyond the limitations of migrant and farm labor; and they joined a new struggle, to obtain an education and a different economic future. César Chávez gave them evidence with his actions that certain change is worthy and necessary.

During the many battles, and power struggles among the growers, the Teamsters, and the United Farm Workers, Chávez was often considered stubborn. It was in the best interests of the growers to control him by changing the balance of power. They expected that if they did, he would be forced to define himself differently. "If we could get the Teamster contract from Chávez," announced Herbert Fleming, President of the Western Growers Association, "then maybe in the long run Chávez would have to shape up and act like a businessman and it would work out."[22] But they underestimated Chávez. His refusal to abandon his convictions made the difference that day. Obviously, he was not going to think "like a businessman" as the growers wanted. From his point of reference, he would think like the people he chose to serve. More importantly, he would think about what would meet their most essential needs as they performed their daily work. An example of this comes in the words of Pacheco:

> That was the 14th of June 1969. César came to Santa Maria to visit us. Before that time, he had only been with us once before. He asked what is going on in Santa Maria and we told him "not much." He told us he wanted us to put toilets in the fields and have fresh water available, so the workers could rest and take a break. So we went to Santa Maria and started talking about the toilets and the people asked what we meant by "toilets." Never before have there been toilets in the fields, not even my grandfather had toilets. We worked real hard; we called it the "Toilet Revolution." We did things peacefully, so we were able to put the toilets up without much resistance. We were able to win that concession. Then the farmers put up more toilets in the fields and gave the workers fresh water. Before this the women had to dig round holes in the ground to take care of their needs.[23]

At a practical level, César Chávez seems to have understood the ethical implications and the consequences for him as the "leader" if he switched his "way of thinking" as the growers would have preferred. Notably, the managerial principles and practices he studied were also part of the tenets that guided him. There seems to have been a major misconception about him as a servant-leader. Although in his humble appearance he might have been perceived solely as a servant, his skills as a leader and manager of a cause gave him the advantage over adversaries who defined themselves solely as "businessmen."

For Chávez, being a man, a servant, and a leader meant more than could be conveyed by the ideas of the "humble Mexican" or the "unyielding Mexican," stereotypical labels that originated in the social structure of the American Southwest in the early twentieth century. Clearly, his advantage of skill and knowledge over his adversaries was often significant. These had been acquired through many years of defiance against the forces of oppression that sought to destroy his true spirit and nature. In the apparent contradiction of the servant-leader, the legacy of César Chávez teaches us about the dichotomous nature of service and leadership. It teaches us about the challenge of being an effective servant-leader while facing our inescapable human frailties.

> Leadership was bestowed on a man who was by nature a servant. It was something given, or assumed, that could be taken away. His servant nature was the real man, not bestowed, not assumed, and not to be taken away. He was a servant first.[24]

Yet César Chávez defined himself simply as someone struggling and praying to be just a man in a world utterly defined by economics, politics, culture, and religion.

Conclusion

> The worst thing that I see is guys who say, "man, they don't have any Chicanos up there [in places of power], and they're not in there working to make sure that it happens. We [as Chicanos] criticize and separate ourselves from the process of change. We've got to jump in there with both feet to change conditions."[25]

César Chávez's life is, among other things, a guide on how to live at the service of others, how to practice leadership at the service of those that are ignored by political and economic structures. Even when criticism arose, his influence was underscored by the unconventionality of his actions in the pursuit of social justice.[26] His life was political because he spoke the unspoken, he defended the humble, the poor, and those left out. He confronted the powerful and the politically untouchable; and he did it while asserting: "Non-violence is our strength."[27] Before Jesse Jackson said "Keep hope alive," Chávez had urged it. Before Jackson called for a Rainbow Coalition, Chávez had formed one. Before the Kennedys discovered the liberal mystique of the poor and poverty, Chávez had lived it and embraced it.[28] And before Robert

K. Greenleaf coined the term *servant-leader* as a conceptual framework for leadership and management, César Chávez had been practicing it.

He presents a paradox: born a man within what some have described as a traditional culture, he nevertheless conducted his life as a human being keenly aware of his connection to all people regardless of background, creed, personal preferences, or opinions. He lived in the paradox of the "borderlands" so aptly described by Gloria Anzaldúa. As a Mexican male, he was surrounded by *las culturas que nos traicionan* (cultures that betray us).[29] César Chávez could have succumbed to its trappings. "Or perhaps...decide to disengage from the dominant culture, write it off altogether as a lost cause, and cross the border into a wholly new and separate territory. Or...go another route."[30] Yet, he seemed to have known, as Anzaldúa concludes: "The possibilities are numerous once we decide to act and not react." He chose to act.

His joys were simple. He derived great pleasure from being with his children, his family, from impromptu hikes with his grandchildren in the hills near La Paz.[31] César, the man, was humble and simple in meaningful ways that his loved ones understood. He was guided by powerful forces—forces that, according to Wheatley, are "the imperative to create one's self as an exploration of newness and the need to reach for relationships with others to create systems."[32] In his life and work, he was ahead of his time and part of a new story for the generations of this century searching for meaning. His words show the depth of his foresight:

> When we are really honest with ourselves, we must admit that our lives are all that really belong to us. So it is how we use our lives that determines what kind of men we are. It is my deepest belief that only by giving our lives do we find life. I am convinced that the truest act of courage, the strongest act of manliness is to sacrifice ourselves for others in a totally non-violent struggle for justice. To be a man is to suffer for others. God help us to be men.[33]

This statement by César Chávez was read to nearly eight thousand farmworkers gathered in Delano on Sunday, March 10, 1968, to break bread with their leader after a twenty-five-day fast for nonviolence.

Our questions about him might teach us more about about ourselves. The questions that emerge from studying the life work of César Chávez as a servant-leader help us focus on a principle of citizenship. His was a type of citizenship that engages with the world; a world where we are aware, and where we assume responsibility for "our capacity to create (do for ourselves) what we had sought from our leaders."[34] Learning from César Chávez's example, and in the still persistent voice of Dolores Huerta, we can answer: Yes, it is possible—*Sí se puede!* It is possible to create and articulate a vision; to be accountable for the well-being of the whole; to set and pursue goals that sustain the institution, so in turn, this institution will sustain us; to establish boundaries and set limits; to create structure and order that suits and sustains our purposes; and to become role models. As we move on to assert our servant-leader spirit, we can begin teaching others. Athie advises us: "It is necessary that the students know that this story was real. In this country, so powerful, so full of beauty, so large, there are also many injustices. We need a Chávez, many Chávezes, so that we can continue doing well for others."[35]

What Are the Implications of this Legacy?

César Chávez's life work teaches us about our responsibility as individuals, to act and create the world of justice we dream of having. In my efforts to preserve this legacy, it is important I reflect upon his life work and ask: What is my responsibility, within a community, to the world we all have created? How can we continue in the legacy of the servant-leader to create a just society for everyone? How do we create and support living systems that sustain all of our differences and similarities. When we discover answers to these questions, we will create living systems where the strength and well-being of those systems is measured by the strength and well-being of each one of its individual members. We will engage in the ongoing dynamics of self-organizing living systems and change the context of politically defined systems that do not serve us well. We will serve well, so that others may be free.

Chapter Three
THE WELCOMING SERVANT-LEADER: THE ART OF CREATING HOSTMANSHIP

Jan Gunnarsson with Olle Blohm

A welcoming servant-leader knows that everyone in an organization contributes in some way to its collective success. What makes welcoming servant-leaders different is that their actions and decisions can have major consequences for the entire organization. As a welcoming servant-leader, you realize that your leadership is expressed by your actions and that you have been instilled with a trust you can't take for granted. I know this sounds like an awesome responsibility, that you'd have to be a superman or superwoman to accomplish it, but I don't believe it is. The hard part is never forgetting the person inside you and always seeing the person in others.

To show you what is needed, I have written down all the qualities of a welcoming leader. After thinking it through, I came up with a list of qualities that I reworded as promises you should be able to make to your employees. They may seem unrealistic at first glance, particularly the last promise, which says you should fulfill all of them every day, but remember that the trust placed in you is rarely based upon what you say as much as what you do.

OK, are you ready?

The Welcoming Leader's Promises

Begin every promise by saying: I am....

1. Accommodating

I see you as the person you are, not one of a multitude.
I try to understand your situation and perspective.
I demonstrate through my thoughts, words, and actions that I
* am accommodating.*

There is no such thing as a finished template. The same words mean different things depending on who is at the receiving end. To be accommodating, you have to adapt your leadership to the situation at hand and understand that a word like *responsibility* is often perceived in different ways.

2. Open

I realize the value of dialogue and listening to one another.
I am open to, and grateful for, your opinions of me and what
* I do.*
I give you all the information you need.
I demonstrate through my thoughts, words, and actions that I
* am open.*

I can't tell you how many times I have heard leaders proudly declare, "My door is always open." The problem is that though their doors may be open, their minds may be closed. Walking into their office is like visiting someone who isn't home.

3. Farsighted

I see opportunities beyond today's problems and challenges.
I act before problems reach me.
I demonstrate through my thoughts, words, and actions that I
* am farsighted.*

Need a property manager? Try looking for someone who has worked on a boat. They know the difference between repairs and maintenance, and know how it feels to be poorly equipped when bad weather strikes. Leaders who can't see beyond the next quarter soon find themselves trying to shake loose after running aground.

In the late twelfth century, a section of Oxford University moved into new buildings. They were very modern for their time, with a chapel and a large hall situated on the north end. In the mid-seventeenth century, nearly five hundred years later, an architect was hired to restore the roof over the hall and discovered that the huge oak beams had begun to rot. The architect and representatives from the university traveled to the Great Hall Woods in Berkshire, where they hoped to find the right wood to replace the beams. How did they know the right wood would be there? Because an anonymous leader had planted trees there a century earlier for that very purpose. That's being farsighted.

4. Empathetic

I am sensitive to your feelings, values, and experiences.
I want to see things from your perspective to understand how
  you can develop as a person.
I demonstrate through my thoughts, words, and actions that I
  empathize.

A little girl in elementary school was stricken by cancer but fortunately recovered after chemotherapy. When she returned to school, her mother tied a bandanna around her head to hide the fact that she had lost her hair. The kids in her class thought it looked funny and teased her. They pulled the bandanna off her head and grew quiet when they saw she had no hair. The girl was heartbroken and ran home in tears. She never wanted to return to school, but her mother soothed her. "They already know," she said. "It's not exciting any longer."

The next morning the children's teacher was wearing a kerchief around her head. When she entered the classroom, she calmly removed it to show that she was completely bald. A week later, all the children in the class had shaved their heads.

5. Ethical

I respect everyone equally.
I try to do what is right, even if it is costly in the short term.
I demonstrate through my thoughts, words, and actions that I
*   am ethical.*

A colonel is called into her general's office. "I've heard that there's going to be a surprise inspection," he told her. "All weapons have to be inspected. Everything has to be in tip-top shape. I suggest we cancel all scheduled exercises and refocus our attention on this instead."

"I can't do that," the colonel said.

"But the inspection is soon, in the next few days."

"That may be."

"We'll be well rewarded."

"Perhaps, but I still can't do it."

"Do you realize what you are saying?"

"I do. I couldn't live with myself knowing that we weren't properly trained. What if we found ourselves in a situation where my soldiers weren't sure how to act? I can't imagine something happening to them just because I wanted a chance at a promotion."

"Are you resisting an order?"

"Yes, I am."

6. Flexible

I realize that my principles are firm, but not so much so that
*   reality won't change them.*
I adapt to situations and act pragmatically.
I demonstrate through my thoughts, words, and actions that I
*   am flexible.*

This is a question of adapting to your surroundings rather than modifying your core beliefs.

Success is rarely the result of what you first had in mind but rather of flexible thinking bordering on the unthinkable. While it has been said that all roads lead to Rome, many people are at a loss when their main route is shut off for as little as an hour.

7. *Generous*

I share my skills, experiences, and talents.
I praise others' ideas, suggestions, and successes.
I am always prepared to take a back seat to benefit others.
I demonstrate through my thoughts, words, and actions that I
*   am generous.*

The best ruler: hardly known to exist.
Next best: known and loved.
Next best: feared.
The worst: despised.
No trust given, no trust received.
The best ruler rules without fanfare.
When his work is successful, the people say,
"Fantastic! We've done it!"[1]

8. *Honest*

I seek the truth, even if it hurts.
I always want you to be honest and straightforward with me.
I demonstrate through my thoughts, words, and actions that I
*   am honest.*

A few years ago, a priest I knew called to tell me proudly that he was joining the "business world." He planned to become an ethics consultant, to use his own life-values to help companies be more ethical. Now he was desperately looking for the right name for his business. He was calling me, he said, because I was a "creative type."

Flattered, I asked him to give me a day to think about it. The next morning the priest-entrepreneur called wondering whether the "creative type" had come up with anything.

"Yep," I said.

"Yep? What?"

"Sincera."

"Sincera?"

"Yep."

"Why Sincera?"

"From the English word, *sincere*, of course."

"I don't want a foreign-sounding name. I'm not planning to go abroad. And besides, what does *sincere* have to do with my little ethical consulting firm?"

"Everything."

"Like what?"

"You know what the word means, don't you?"

"Yes. Honest, true, or something along those lines."

"Exactly. Or perhaps I should say *sincerely*. According to a widespread folk etymology, it is a compound word actually, combining *sin*, meaning without—you know, like *sin gas*, without bubbles, like at the cafés in Las Palmas."

"OK, and…?"

"The second part of the word, -*cere*, comes from *cera*, and means 'wax.'"

"Wax!?"

"Yeah. It has been said that in Roman times, marble was sold in the marketplace. Most stones had cracks of one size or another. Some salespersons tried to hide them by filling the cracks with wax so they couldn't be seen. The more honest ones, on the other hand, those with ethics and morals, sold the stones as is, without wax—*sin ceres*. Thus, the word *sincere*. Not so bad for a company in ethics consulting."

"Better than you think. I have just rented a room in one of those old marble buildings in town."

9. Humble

I realize I can't see and know everything.

I understand that your perspective is valuable and makes us all better.

I avoid using my power to convince you.

I don't let my success stop me from being a welcoming leader.

*I demonstrate through my thoughts, words, and actions that I
am humble.*

When Mr. Know-It-All joins a new company, he asks:
"What do I have to do?"
A humble leader will ask:
"What has to be done?"

10. *Clear*

I seek simplicity in everything we do.
*I always try to express myself in a way that can't be misinter-
preted.*
*I demonstrate through my thoughts, words, and actions that I
am clear.*

At a staff meeting, my assistant Monica was asked to present
to our employees a quality survey we had recently conducted.

Monica stepped up to the microphone and said, "Today we're
going to show you something very exciting, a PDS survey that
we...."

"A what?" someone shouted from the audience.

"It's called a PDS survey," she said, spelling it out.

"Whaddya mean PDS?"

"PDS stands for Problem Detection Study."

"Tell us something we can understand," another person
shouted.

"Well, it means...a survey to identify problems."

There was another shout from the audience: "Haven't you
figured out all the problems already?"

"Why can't you folks on the board speak so we can understand?" asked someone else.

"We're not on the board. We're part of the management team."

"Same thing. We want to understand what you're talking
about."

Clarity matters.

11. *Aware*

I know myself and feel confident when interacting with others.
I choose to leave my personal problems outside work and not
*   infect those around me.*
I reflect about myself and the way I am.
I demonstrate through my thoughts, words, and actions that I
*   am aware.*

Once there was a man who visited a guru to learn the meaning of life. He was invited to tea, sat down and began to talk. The guru took the teapot and filled the man's cup, but wouldn't stop pouring. The tea ran over the table and onto the floor until the man saw what was happening and asked, "What are you doing? Can't you see that it's already full?"

"If you are going to learn something new," the guru said, "you have to leave the room for it. If your cup is already full, there's no point."

I once attended a course in which they taught us to be more aware. In one exercise, we were each asked to list fifteen to twenty qualities that characterized us, as opposed to coming up with personal "brands" that we thought might make us more marketable or popular. When I returned home, this list of qualities convinced me to quit my job. I had left the course with a greater awareness of who I was, and I knew that I no longer wanted to continue to do what I was doing.

Writer Julia Cameron has suggested three ways to be more perceptive and creative. She calls the first "The Morning Papers," which entails sitting down each morning to write three pages in longhand about whatever comes to mind. The second is called "The Artist Date," to set aside time once a week for yourself. And the third is "The Artist Walk," which is a long walk to clear your head.

All of us want to be leaders who have a strong sense of self, who don't pretend to be someone else. And you know what… our employees hope for the same thing.

12. *Supportive*

> *I give you support and help you avoid obstacles.*
> *I am here for you, especially when times are tough.*
> *I demonstrate through my thoughts, words, and actions that I*
>   *am supportive.*

When asked how his company had changed after growing from just a few employees to thirty-four thousand, Herb Kelleher of Southwest Airlines replied that it hadn't. The foundation was the same. They continue to stress that their employees are people. No matter what happens in their lives—whether they are celebrating or grieving, having children or struggling with a personal loss or serious illness, the company contacts them by phone, by letter, or by doing something memorable. To this day, they still tell employees the same thing: We are with you and we care about the whole you, not just the part we see on weekdays between eight in the morning and five in the evening.

Those are the words of a man whose company didn't even report a financial loss or fire any employees after September 11, 2001. A man who has built a business where the employees are always priority number one.

13. *Trustful*

> *I know that the word trust can be interpreted in different ways.*
> *I know that trust takes years to earn, but can be lost in a day.*
> *I demonstrate through my thoughts, words, and actions that I*
>   *am trustful.*

Mutual trust is characteristic of all relationships. Leadership is built totally on trust. If we lose it, we lose everything and can no longer serve. To serve is to rely on people. You have to be willing to step aside and rely on others to make the right choices, even if they aren't the same ones you would make.

The trust we feel is revealed in how we see our fellow human beings: whether we see others as good, generous, and altruistic or mean-spirited, greedy, and egotistical. Our view of humanity is critical to how we lead and create our businesses. There is a big difference between creating structures and systems based on control and building them on trust.

14. *Appreciative*

> *I appreciate that I may serve you and others.*
> *I express my appreciation for your efforts.*
> *I appreciate that you criticize me and what I do.*
> *I demonstrate through my thoughts, words, and actions that I am appreciative.*

If we had to make it in the world being able to say only one word, it should be *thanks*. That will get you far.

All leaders should spend time in their organizations reminding themselves of everything they should be thankful for. Or they should begin each meeting by thanking someone in the group. This is a lot better than going around looking for faults, which can be extremely stressful.

Thanking an employee for having chosen to work for your organization isn't unusual today. What is important is that the person who says it also really believes it. So, take out a piece of paper and write down the top ten people who deserve your gratitude. Who is on the top of the list? Second, third, fourth...?

15. *Demanding*

> *I want to get so many things done and place high demands on my work and myself.*
> *I follow your work and development.*
> *I convince you not to worry about failure and think along new lines.*
> *I demonstrate through my thoughts, words, and actions that I am demanding.*

In *Man and Superman*, George Bernard Shaw wrote,

This is the one true joy in my life. That is of being used for a purpose, and that I recognize the deed as a mighty one; and of being a part of a force of nature and not just a feverish, selfish little clod of ailments and grievances complaining that the world will not devote itself to keeping me happy. I want to be thoroughly used up when I die, for the harder I work the more I live. I rejoice in life for its own sake. Life is no "brief candle" for me. It is a sort of splendid torch which I have gotten hold of for the moment, and I want to make it burn as brightly as possible before handing it on to the next man.[2]

16. Knowledgeable

I understand the logic and context of what we are working to achieve.
I can perform the duties entrusted to me.
I am always interested in learning.
I demonstrate through my thoughts, words, and actions that I am knowledgeable.

Knowledge comes from understanding what transpires with guests. It's seeing things as they really are without interfering or trying to control what's happening. Spend a day in a store. Follow a home delivery. See for yourself the problems and challenges your employees face on a daily basis.

It is easy to buy surveys and send out consultants to your offices to find out the "truth." But technically, only the leader can seek out knowledge.

17. Foresighted

I think about the consequences of our decisions in the long term.
I am always aware of the responsibility I bear for our collective future.
I demonstrate through my thoughts, words, and actions that I am foresighted.

A chicken farmer once told me that good hens lay one egg a day—no more, no less. To get them to produce more, some farmers try to shorten the hens' day using lights, so they believe a day has twenty-three or sometimes even twenty-two hours.

"There's a limit," he said. "But a friend of mine got so carried away he kept cutting the time shorter and shorter. He called me to boast that he was down to nineteen hours. But then a few of his hens seemed to fight back, to go on strike, and they stopped laying eggs altogether. The farmer began to panic and cut the time even shorter, until one morning he woke up to find all his hens dead."

18. Decisive

I address issues and problems and don't avoid them.
I often make decisions without being one hundred percent sure how they will turn out.
I realize that sometimes it is better to correct decisions than to never make them.
I demonstrate through my thoughts, words, and actions that I am decisive.

For something to happen, I cannot wait forever.
For something to happen, I cannot wait until everyone says yes.
For something to happen, I have to make mistakes sometimes.
For something to happen, I have to be willing to take a slap on the wrist once in awhile.
For something to happen, I have to be a little more daring than others.
For something to happen, I cannot keep looking in the rearview mirror.
For something to happen, I have to realize that not everyone sees things the same way I do.
For something to happen, I have to let intuition guide me.
For something to happen, I have to risk much of what I have today.

For something to happen, I have to be prepared for
    taunts from those who stand still.

I must otherwise accept the shame of not having done
    anything.
In the end, time is merely the sum of everything that
    has taken place.
And the person who judges it.
Which means me.

—Jan Gunnarsson, written by the
Ullån brook in Sweden, 1992

19. Optimistic

I believe everything is possible until someone has proven other-
    wise.
I am driven by the idea of a successful conclusion.
I demonstrate through my thoughts, words, and actions that I
    am optimistic.

The wind has subsided. The ship lies still. The crew gathers in
the cold.

"What did I tell you?" says Whiner. "We should have steered
in the other direction."

"I'm getting out of here," says Shark Bait, who dives into the
water and disappears.

All the while, the captain poetically contemplates the winds
that await, the spray of saltwater, and the challenges ahead,
adjusting the rigging to take advantage of the wind whenever it
happens to arrive.

20. Curious

I am always searching for ways to serve better.
I look for problems to solve and needs to fill.
I look for the right questions, not just the right answers.

*I demonstrate through my thoughts, words, and actions that I
am curious.*

All that glitters is not gold. Sometimes it can be worth much
more.

Inventors typically love to hear phrases such as, "That's never
been done," "That's not possible," or "You can't do that." That
only fuels the fire burning inside an innovator on the hunt for
problems to solve and needs to satisfy.

All businesses exist to fill a need and solve a problem people
have. This is supposed to be reflected in their mission statement.
Winners usually see a need arise and solve the problem before
others do. But if you spend all your time on solutions, you run the
risk of falling behind and watching the backs of your competitors.

21. Proud

I am proud of you and show it.
I try to limit myself to doing things we can be proud of.
*I demonstrate through my thoughts, words, and actions that I
am proud.*

I once met Bill George, the former Chairman and CEO of
Medtronic, who offered me the following advice on being a true
welcoming leader:
Be motivated by your job, not by money.
Be guided by your values, not your ego.
Share with others what is inside you, not just your outside.
Live your life with enough discipline that you would be proud
to see yourself on the front page of the newspaper.
"It's no harder than that," he said with a smile.

22. Responsible

*I take responsibility for how I relate to everything that happens
to me.*

*I shoulder ultimate responsibility for what I have done and the
decisions I have made.*
*I take responsibility that you will be able to handle the duties I
have entrusted to you.*
*I demonstrate through my thoughts, words, and actions that I
am responsible.*

Responsibility can also mean the "ability to respond." While
it would be impossible to hold you responsible for everything
that can happen, you are always responsible for how you react to
what has happened. Taking responsibility means facing any situation without switching to autopilot or sweeping problems under
the rug.

23. Devoted

*I realize what we are trying to achieve together is the most
important thing.*
*I want us to be willing to go off the beaten track when reality
says otherwise.*
*I demonstrate through my thoughts, words, and actions that I
am devoted.*

One day I was walking in the city with my eight-year-old son
when the following transpired: we were standing at a crosswalk
waiting for the light to turn green. As soon as it changed, he took
a step into the street. Out of the side of my eye, I saw a bus coming full speed, so I reached out to grab him and pulled him back
to safety. The bus brushed against his jacket and sped around the
corner.

A combination of fear and anger came over me as I grabbed
him by the shoulders and screamed, "What are you doing! You
could have been killed. You have to look before you cross the
street."

My son looked up at me in surprise and said, "But Dad, you
told me that I can walk when the light turns green."

"You have to look first."

"But the light was green."

We teach our kids to obey and trust the system. But if someone else breaks the rules, they are the ones who risk being run over.

Being law-abiding is of little help when circumstances require us to act differently.

24. Passionate

I feel strongly about what we are working together to achieve.
I see this passion for what we are doing as an important fuel for our company's development.
I demonstrate through my thoughts, words, and actions that I am passionate.

One day a worried accountant walked into a leader's office and said, "Things are looking bad. We'll soon have no money left."

"How fortunate, I thought you were going to say we had no more ideas," he replied. "Without ideas, no amount of money will help us. Good ideas always manage to attract the money they need."

A few weeks later, the head of development came to his office and said, "We've got a big problem. It appears we've run out of ideas."

"I see," the leader replied. "But we should be happy we still have courage. Without the courage to get things done, no ideas in the world are going to help us. With courage, we will certainly develop new ideas that will attract the money to put them into action."

After a few months, a worried HR manager came into his office and said, "It's hopeless. We've lost our courage. This is the end."

The leader replied, "As long as we have our passion and dreams, the end is not near. Because without passion, our courage won't be enough to create good ideas that will attract the resources needed to make them a reality. You can't extract apples from a tree. They come when the tree is willing to bear fruit."

25. *Silent*

*I understand the importance of silence, so my words don't get
in the way.*
I realize we must all think through what we are going to say.
*I demonstrate through my thoughts, words, and actions that I
can be silent.*

It's an art to refrain from conveying wisdom. To avoid being
the "answering machine" people have come to expect. Being
silent is about pacing. You have to hold your tongue at the right
moments and for the right length of time. Surveys have shown
that people who are slightly quieter than others often lead successful businesses. Personally, I have a hard time shutting up, so
much so that I once forced myself to visit a retreat where we had
to remain silent for fourteen days. ("Dear God," my mother said.
"How will you manage that? I don't think I could be quiet for
fourteen seconds, and you inherited it.") After a fortnight of
silence, I returned to reality at the airport in Nice and then later
at the company I worked for.

What a cacophony!

Not everyone needs a retreat to find silence. You can always
watch the sunset, as people used to do, sitting quietly together as
darkness falls and reflecting on the day that has passed and the
one to come.

26. *Consistent*

*I realize that I must renew my promises every day, in every
encounter and every decision.*
I want to serve as an example.
*I demonstrate my consistency through my thoughts, words, and
actions.*

There you have them, twenty-six promises of a welcoming
leader. Are you willing to let your colleagues rate them as either
Important, Fairly important, or Unimportant? Ask them to make
life a little easier for you by crossing a few off the list?

Which ones do you think they will choose?
Which would you choose yourself?
No heroes, please.

Finally, another maxim on the paradoxes of leadership: The less you lead, the stronger your leadership.

It is not heroes we need but hosts. People who make everyone—employees, guests, partners and owners—feel welcome. Hosts who realize that leadership is like driving a snow plow; you keep the streets clean so others can move about freely.

Hostmanship is the decisive difference. In a world where everything looks similar—products and places, companies and countries—a guest or employee makes his decisions based on how welcome he feels. To provide hostmanship we have to trust our human nature and the human side of our businesses. We must rejoice in serving others and offer leadership that reflects this.

True change requires change at the deepest level—in your soul. Democracy, as we know, is more a matter of what people think and do than what our elected officials manage to accomplish. As welcoming servant-leaders, we must give strength to those around us, give substance to our collective search for meaning, and give satisfaction to the many people we are in a position to serve. We do so by weaning our employees off "leadership dependency," freeing our organizations, starting conversations, and building arenas for communication. We must encourage them to voluntarily rise from their stools, climb down from the bleachers, and join the game instead of offering sensible advice from the sidelines. All the while, we, as servant-leaders, have to remove the halo from our heads and replace it with welcoming leadership that recognizes the human side of those we meet.

Chapter Four
THE MANAGEMENT DEVELOPMENT LEGACY OF ROBERT K. GREENLEAF
Jeff McCollum and Joel Moses

Robert Greenleaf's writings have inspired considerable thought and his name will forever be linked with "servant-leadership"—something he wrote extensively about in his second career as author and consultant. Greenleaf's first career, the thirty-eight years he spent with AT&T, produced a rich legacy of innovation. At that time, the official name of the company was American Telephone and Telegraph, but throughout this article, we will use AT&T, the contemporary identification. In Greenleaf's work at AT&T, we can find the antecedents to contemporary development endeavors such as coaching, "action learning," and assessment centers. Although his writing on servant-leadership has been reviewed in considerable detail, relatively little has been written regarding his impact on business and the legacy he left as Director of Management Research at AT&T. This chapter, which focuses on the assessment center in theory and practice, is designed to help fill this void.

Greenleaf's work at AT&T integrated three broad thematic elements in his life. He began his formal college education by studying engineering at Rose Polytechnic in Terre Haute, Indiana. After a time spent in construction, he enrolled in Carleton College where Oscar Helming, a sociology professor, challenged his students to get inside a large institution and make it more responsive to serving the public good. In a humorous and elegant irony that harkens back to his days as a laborer, Greenleaf's own epitaph reads, "Potentially a good plumber, ruined by a sophisticated education."

Taking up Helming's challenge, Greenleaf started work with Ohio Bell. As was typical of college graduates who were being indoctrinated into the Bell System at the time, he started as a laborer on a construction crew. He quickly moved into a training role and asked to lead foreman conferences. Greenleaf describes this period as "the most formative experience in his adult life." During this experience, he began to think of himself as a "student of organization." From Ohio, he moved to AT&T's corporate staff in New York, specifically to the operations and engineering department. In 1941, he was appointed head of AT&T's management development section.

Practicality and applied science drove much of what he did. Today that orientation is coming back into the leadership/development literature as "evidence based management." Colleagues at AT&T, remember him as "practical and focused, shunning what could be seen as academic." Although much of what is written about Greenleaf today creates a quality of *eminent grise* around him, his AT&T work focused on how things work and how to make them work better by applying the findings of work in academe.

This clearly emerges in his work with assessment centers. The technology, applied to specific business problems confronting AT&T, originated in the military during World War II, but Greenleaf was able to take this technique and apply it to the world of business. Greenleaf's interest in how people develop and mature spawned a thirty-year research effort, the Management Progress Study, within AT&T.

The study built upon work begun within AT&T in the late 1920s. The fact that any company undertook such a study in the 1950s and committed to it for thirty years stands as a testament to a much more stable business environment and Greenleaf's ability to influence. The study ended when AT&T divested its operating telephone companies in 1984 to end its antitrust suit with the U.S. government.[1]

Background of the Management Progress Study

Recognizing that a major source of leadership talent could be attracted and retained by identifying college graduates and gradually exposing them to the workings of the telephone company, in the 1920s the Bell System began one of the first comprehensive studies to evaluate the success of college hires. Coincidentally, this study began at about the same time Bob Greenleaf joined AT&T from Ohio Bell but also paralleled many of his later work achievements.

The recruitment study tracked over 3,800 college hires and pointed out that college grades and class standing could predict salary and job success. Beginning with a trickle of managers in the 1920s, over 2,000 college recruits were hired annually by the mid-1950s. While some of these recruits would pursue careers as technical specialists and scientists, most were expected to enter management roles and rise to middle and eventually upper levels in the Bell System. By the time Greenleaf came to AT&T's headquarters in New York City, a thriving program had been developed to both attract and retain this talent.

In the early 1950s a pioneering development program that exposed promising high potential managers to a liberal arts curriculum was initiated at the University of Pennsylvania. Historically, this university had been one of the early pioneers in the young field of applied psychology, beginning with a seminal study on the selection of salesmen in the early 1900s. By the time Greenleaf had become director of management research, this program had drawn young managers to a yearlong liberal arts curriculum. Proving too costly and unwieldy for the Bell System companies, a series of shorter programs were initiated at Dartmouth, Williams, and Greenleaf's alma mater, Carleton College. These programs were the first serious attempts at broadening the perspectives of managers by exposing them to new ideas and a broader outlook than had been provided in their previous technical training. Today, continuing education programs based on this model are de rigueur for colleges and businesses.

These programs continued for many years, shaping the development of high potential managers and were formalized as part of an Initial Management Development Program (IMDP) formed under Greenleaf's stewardship. Although young college managers became a major source of management talent, little was known about the factors that shaped their development. To better understand how AT&T and the Bell System developed these programs, we must first look at the seminal study that Greenleaf sponsored, the AT&T Management Progress Study.

The Management Progress Study

The roots of the Management Progress Study, a twenty-five-year longitudinal study of managerial lives, began during World War II. The Office of Strategic Services (OSS) under General Bill Donovan was responsible for selecting spies who could be introduced into Europe to assist resistance leaders fighting the Germans. Donovan's team turned to one of the very early American psychoanalysts, Dr. Henry Murray. Murray, a contemporary of Freud, focused on the conscious rather than unconscious determinants of personality. During the late 1920s he initiated groundbreaking research in the emerging field of personality development at his clinic at Harvard University, research he described in a landmark book, *Explorations in Personality*, published in 1938.

As the United States was entering the war, Murray and his associates were commissioned to develop a special training school to select and train spies. They designed a series of exercises and simulations to screen candidates and over 5,300 officers, enlisted personnel, and civilian volunteers participated in this process. After World War II, the results of this effort became public in a 1946 *Fortune* article entitled "A Good Man Is Hard To Find," while more substantive details were provided in a book authored by Murray and the OSS assessment staff, *The Assessment of Men*, published in 1948.

Greenleaf brought this book and the *Fortune* article to the attention of AT&T's senior leadership during the 1950s, noting that while psychologists knew something about child development, little was known about how adults developed, particularly those entering business. Eventually Greenleaf received executive support for a highly visionary project that would dramatically change our understanding of leadership selection and development.

To head up this study, Greenleaf hired a young researcher, Doug Bray. Bray held a PhD from Yale, and was working at Columbia University on one of the many studies that came out of the personnel research generated during World War II. Building on the assessment exercises and simulations developed by the OSS, Bray and his colleagues launched the pioneering study that eventually shaped much of today's leadership practices.

Four hundred and twenty two young managers were studied, beginning with a sample of Michigan Bell managers in the summer of 1956. The study participants either were brand new college recruits hired into one of the Bell companies participating in the study, or were high-potential high school graduates who had started as craft workers and had been rapidly promoted to the first level of management.

To get a perspective on their leadership capabilities, each participant was assessed at a specially created one-week assessment center, where twenty-five specific management attributes were evaluated (see Appendix). The assessment staff was composed of psychologists and managers who observed the participants and made these ratings. At the conclusion of each program, each participant was rated regarding his potential to reach middle management. As a research program, these results were not shared with either the individual or his management.

Following the assessment, yearly follow-up interviews were conducted with the participant and his management to assess career progress and to learn about their work and nonwork activities. Eight years after the initial assessment, the group was reassessed in a parallel assessment center, again without feedback provided to either the participants or their management. A third assessment center was conducted for those with the company twenty years after the initial assessment. Since the assessment results would have no material impact on their careers at this stage in their lives, the findings were shared with the participants and feedback was provided, enabling a rich review of their career progress. The results of this landmark study have been published extensively and have had an important impact on the identification and development of managers.

Two major, but divergent streams of knowledge emerged from this study and we shall consider each. From a developmental perspective, the key learnings during a manager's formative years were seen to make a significant impact on career success. At the same time, techniques that could accurately assess and predict subsequent talent were developed and put into place.

The Development of Managers

A key driver of the Management Progress Study was Greenleaf's insistence on identifying those factors that led to success in business. Along with this, he wanted to develop and install practices that would directly contribute to the development of talent. Although he believed, as most did at the time, that education was the primary precursor to success, Greenleaf also anticipated research, which would emerge many decades later, that indicated that job experiences were also crucial, and at times, even more critical to management and executive development.

One of the most interesting findings of the Management Progress Study was that career progress varied among the managers who were all assessed as having middle-management potential—ranging from little to exceptionally rapid upward promotional movement. In analyzing the data, a key finding emerged. Enriched career experience in the form of more challenging job assignments early in one's career seemed to make a great deal of difference in the lives of these managers. Those, for example, given early job responsibility for independent action or encouraging early career visibility, seemed to progress faster and further regardless of their assessed potential.

Building on this research, and continuing the earlier legacy of providing high-potential managers a liberal arts education, Greenleaf and his associates developed a highly innovative development program, the Initial Management Development Program. This program, eventually widely copied by most of industry, provided a framework for development during their formative years in the company.

Participants in the program were hired with the expectation that they would reach middle levels of management quickly—in ten years or less, a rate of progress that, in the Bell System of the 1960s, was considered exceptionally rapid. Those not progressing at a pace comparable to their peers were either dropped from the program or terminated from the company. As such, it was a high-risk, high-reward program. To aid in their development, rotational assignments were provided and monitored. Managers were exposed to several different departments during their first two to eight years in business, affording them a wide exposure both to leaders in different organizational settings as well as a perspective on broader business issues. Along with the rotational program, formal training was provided, either derivatives of the liberal arts programs noted above or company-sponsored programs using college faculty.

The Initial Management Development Program continued for many years following Greenleaf's retirement in 1964. It paved the way for enriching the development of thousands of managers in the Bell System, and by its adoption by virtually every major U.S. corporation in some form or another, the development of literally the next generation of business leaders. Integrating classroom learning with on-the-job developmental experiences, it served as a valuable adjunct to more formal educational experiences initially provided by a few business schools that eventually spawned an entire industry of adult development.

The Selection of Managers

One of the more significant findings of the Management Progress Study was the strong correlation between predictions made by the assessment center staff regarding further managerial potential, and the actual progress of these managers. This led to another of Greenleaf's pioneering legacies—the use of assessment centers to select and develop managers.

For those not familiar with the workings of an assessment center, its process is designed to ensure the objectivity and standardization of judgments about potential. Used for both selection and development, participants engage in activities not normally observed on the current job, but which are critical for more demanding assignments at higher levels in the organization. To measure performance, behavioral simulations that mirror issues faced by the host organization are used. These consist of individual and group problem-solving tasks; individual and group analytic exercises along with special interviews; interactive exercises with customers, subordinates, or peers; and other specially constructed activities that reflect the behavioral demands in the target assignment. A team of professional assessors consisting of managers or psychologists trained to apply these techniques observes the participant's performance. A typical center lasts from one to three days, with feedback to both the participant and his or her management that provides targeted developmental actions based on performance during the center. As of today, millions of participants have been assessed worldwide, with considerable research documenting the fairness and accuracy of this technique.

Returning to the Management Progress Study for a moment to learn more about the origins of this technique illuminates another facet of Greenleaf's sponsorship of ideas. Applied research typically looks for immediate translation of scientific findings to practice, often contaminating what may be exceptionally valuable insights in management's zeal to use a promising process that can quickly enhance business results. Longitudinal research, spanning decades, minimizes these problems but is both costly and exceptionally hard to sell in a forward-moving business environment. To Greenleaf's credit, he was able to convince senior management of the long-term benefits of conducting such a study, with the result that among behavioral research conducted over the last hundred years, the Management Progress Study stands out as one of the luminary events in the development of managers.

Since the findings of this research had not been shared with either the participants or their management, these findings became even more powerful. There had been no contamination of results that could have either inadvertently or directly affected their progress. In this way, the validity of the assessment center method was initially established.

Well before the study results were obtained, however, there was considerable interest in this technique, and Greenleaf and his associates were able to parley the need for rapid implementation of new processes while keeping the study viable for over twenty-five years. Managers visiting the Management Progress Study Assessment Center asked whether the process could be modified from a research to an operational program, and in 1958, the first business application used for the selection of foremen was instituted. Ultimately, over the course of the next decades, over 200,000 men and women would participate in one of the Bell System's fifty operational assessment centers established throughout the United States.

Greenleaf also encouraged "giving science away" and the researchers at AT&T quickly shared their knowledge with contemporaries in other organizations. Companies such as IBM, Standard Oil (now BP), and Sears were among the first after AT&T to adopt this process. By 1969, there was such considerable interest in this technique that a group of researchers and practitioners formed the Assessment Center Research Group, which not only shared practices but also created a set of ethical standards concerning the use of assessment centers that have since been adopted by the field.

Applications moved from business to education, and the first widespread use of assessment centers as a key element in an educational curriculum was established at Alverno College in Milwaukee, a nationally recognized Catholic liberal arts college for women. Greenleaf had extensive interaction with Alverno, specifically its president, Sister Joel Read, who, in turn, pioneered radical ideas like learning contracts between the college and the student.

A very interesting sidelight links Greenleaf's role across many diverse institutions. Key leaders of Alverno, including its president, Sister Read (who eventually became a board member of the Greenleaf Center for Servant-Leadership), came to AT&T to learn about this technique. Coincidently, the first of the AT&T books describing the Management Progress Study, *Formative Years in Business*, had just been published with its dedication to Robert Greenleaf. The Alverno team pointed out how Greenleaf's

94

Servant-Leadership was a key inspirational reading in their order, quickly cementing the bond between the AT&T staff and, particularly, these authors, to creating a continuing relationship with this institution for almost thirty years.

As assessment centers continued to be used in both educational and business settings, considerable research evolved regarding the value of this technique, including the landmark book, *Applying the Assessment Center Method*.[2] Eventually this technique received considerable academic credence, and over a thousand scientific and technical studies have been published worldwide.

There are assessment centers used in every continent in the world, in diverse settings such as business, education, government, law, and professional practice. It has become one of the most dominant and widely respected techniques for identifying and developing talent—largely due to the pioneering vision of Robert Greenleaf. From this perspective, an important insight becomes readily apparent: the powerful extension of Greenleaf's foresight regarding human development and the nature of talent now accompanies the daily life of businesses and other organizations throughout the world.

The Empowerment of Managers

Greenleaf's impact on the practice of selecting and developing managers emerged through his role at AT&T during a critical period as the company emerged as one of the premier business leaders of the twentieth century. Although he provided the leadership spark, his efforts came to fruition in part due to his capacity to select a team of researchers who could implement and expand on his ideas, but also in part due to the trust and respect he earned with AT&T's key business leaders.

However, a more enduring contribution, directly associated with Greenleaf, is the concept of empowerment. Derived from his writings about servant-leadership, empowerment focuses on creating a work climate where diverse ideas are both respected and encouraged. Hierarchical organizations, built on the military model of the 1900s and stressing rigid organizational structures with clear spans of control, have given way to less formal structures that focus more on leaders providing the resources for work to get done via a span of support.

The Bell System of Greenleaf's era was a stable bureaucracy with clearly defined management roles, a set of operating procedures, and considerable standardization. Working within this framework, Greenleaf anticipated many of the social and organizational changes that mirror today's global workplace. In our view, his work correctly anticipated significant changes that have been taking place in organizations. Bartlett and Ghoshal (2002) have described the strategic shift from a focus on financial resources (1970s and 1980s) to organizational capability in the late 1980s and early 1990s to a focus on human and intellectual capital.[3] Greenleaf's focus on development of human capital was radical when he was writing. It has been estimated that it takes a generation for a true innovation to become commonplace. Greenleaf's innovations in management development have helped shape the work of all of us working in the field today.

Robert Greenleaf emerged as one of the key leaders in the areas of management education, selection, and development. Characteristically modest, he left it to others to write and expand on his seminal ideas. His direct impact on the role of liberal arts education in business by stressing that development is a lifelong process that matters, spawned today's market for adult education—both through company-sponsored advanced management programs as well as through many university-based learning initiatives. His role in establishing the Management Progress Study demonstrated how managers actually develop over time, as well as the role of assessment centers as a viable selection technique that encourages rigorous selection and development practices.

Finally, the concept of empowerment is directly attributable to his writings and in this manner, Greenleaf left a major mark on contemporary business practices—in leadership and in the development of human capital, but as importantly, in creating the types of corporate cultures that in today's world are key bridges of international success.

Appendix: Management Progress Study Variables

This appendix lists the variables associated with the process of finding and developing future leaders at AT&T. As such, in this list, touched with Greenleaf's profound vision and his taste for nuance and discernment, we find not only the antecedents to contemporary development endeavors such as coaching, "action learning," and assessment centers, but also the antecedents to what would later become Greenleaf's formulation of servant-leadership itself.

Scholastic Aptitude (General Mental Ability)
Oral Communication Skill
Human Relations Skills
Personal Impact
Perception of Threshold Social Cues
Creativity
Self-Objectivity
Social Objectivity
Behavior Flexibility
Need Approval of Superiors
Need Approval of Peers
Inner Work Standards
Need Advancement
Need Security
Goal Flexibility
Primacy of Work
Bell System Value Orientation
Realism of Expectations
Tolerance of Uncertainty
Ability to Delay Gratification
Resistance to Stress
Range of Interests
Energy
Organization and Planning
Decision Making[4]

Chapter Five

COACHING FOR SERVANT-LEADERSHIP: EXPANDING THE CAPACITY TO REFLECT FROM THE HEART

Deborah V. Welch with
Virginia Duncan Gilmore

Caring is an exacting and demanding business. It
requires not only interest and compassion and concern;
it demands self-sacrifice and wisdom and tough-
mindedness and discipline.[1]

—Robert Greenleaf

Maureen Baginski, director of one of the U.S. Security
Agency's main missions, wakes up each morning to the awesome
responsibility of leadership for our nation's security. In an auditorium filled with 200 Phoenix business leaders just after the
September 11 attack, I heard Maureen speak on the importance of
self-development and creating a workplace where people can
learn openly rather than try to hide their individual "deficiencies." I felt myself breathe a sigh of relief to learn that a wise servant-leader is at the helm of an agency in charge of tracking
global nuclear weapons. We are all so vulnerable.

Most of us who are a part of this growing servant-leadership
movement wake up in the morning with many important responsibilities. Whether our responsibilities are for global safety, our
organization's bottom line, or our family's well-being, leadership

is vital and complex work. We have to balance a high vision with the day-to-day work of what is possible. Every day we face the reality of hundreds of e-mails, phone calls, and long lists of activities to do. Yet somehow, we also need to pay attention to the quality of our lives. In those moments when things seem unclear or overwhelming and impossible to balance, the hardest task may be to sit still, reflect, and ask ourselves the question Greenleaf suggested: "How can I use myself to best serve today?"

This essay will offer some ways to use coaching as a vehicle for reflection and for the development of servant-leadership capacities. In it, I will share some of the important concepts I have discovered in both my research of servant-leaders who build high trust cultures and in my coaching work—particularly my coaching partnership with Virginia Duncan Gilmore.

We will begin with the concept of *reflection.*

What Is Reflection?

Reflection is an increasing awareness of thoughts and feelings that allows a person to see things in a new light and more complete light. Greenleaf proposed that we must develop the ability to withdraw and reorient ourselves, if only for a moment, to sort out the most important from the less important. At its most basic level, reflection is taking time to think. We certainly need to think back on our experience, as doing so can create foresight directed toward a better future.

Reflection can move beyond merely thinking to *thinking about our thinking.* Greg Merton, vice-president at Hewlett-Packard, is one example of a person who employs the capacity of "thinking about thinking" to develop deeper understandings and processes. Greg led one of the most successful technology and business ventures in the history of HP—the inkjet division. He used reflective practices in leadership as his division grew from 75 to 10,000 employees globally. At the time of the most dramatic change in his division during the early 1990s, Greg expanded his reflection on the organization's social system by introducing living systems as a fresh way of thinking about thinking. "It's very clear in the physical world that we can't make inkjet cartridges while violating the laws of Mother Nature," he observed, "yet we often act as if we can decide what works in the social world rather than discover and abide by the laws in that arena as well." Greg met with his staff one day a month with two coaches to, in his words, "take on personal growth, team effectiveness and leadership."[2]

The dimensions of thinking can go still deeper than thinking about one's thinking. We also need to connect to the heart. Sometimes deep reflection is confused with increasing the intensity of intellectual analysis, but increasingly complex analysis may not get us to the place of greatest vision and deepest understanding and wisdom. So, do we *think* our way into the heart? No, we shift perspective.

Picture a beautiful mountain lake on a calm day. The water is still and offers a perfect, crystal-clear reflection of a mountain. You see the lake differently depending upon whether you look with an objective eye, a critical eye, or a poetic eye. You might glance only briefly, and then move on with a "to do" list. Or, you might use the opportunity to be still and dip deeply into a profound experience of nature's beauty. The water in the lake further reflects deeper places within each of us, just like the depths of reflection where you can hear the callings of your heart.

Or what Parker Palmer calls the "heart's imperatives."[3]

Virginia Duncan Gilmore reflects on one of her earliest calls to be a servant-leader:

> One story that forever remains in my heart goes back to a time in my family business, Kaytee Products. Our organization was working to facilitate teamwork throughout the company. I was asked to lead a task force to help our company work together better. For a year we worked to become a team ourselves. We drew a new organizational chart of interconnected circles, designed around processes rather than departments. After a year of training and shared learning, a special group of people from many different departments met with our task force. They told us what this experience had meant for them. They talked about why it was important in their work and why it was important to them as individuals. I remember one person

talking who hardly ever expressed herself before, and there was a new radiance in her presence. As she talked I could feel the energy moving in my body and my heart opening. The message shot through my being—that there could be a better way to work and that the workplace could and needed to be life giving for human beings. I knew I would never be the same. The promise of that day in my life lives on in my heart and calls me every day, especially on the days that are more challenging than others.

If you connect to more than your intellect, if you include your heart when you reflect, you will hear your heart's call, just like Virginia. You will have an opportunity for clarity in your direction and, therefore, renewal.

How Reflection Is Practiced

Before continuing with Virginia's story, it is important to consider the ways reflection is practiced. The disciplines of reflection include dialogue and coaching practices as well as contemplation from many traditions. Here are some quotes from senior leaders describing how they listen to their inner wisdom, their spirit, their heart.

Jim Stewart:

Sometimes as a leader you can undergo a swirling torrent of pressures and attacks. But there's a place of stillness in the storm. Getting to a place of stillness allows miraculous things to come out of you and show up around you. I go into the garden, because that is where I am happiest, I clear my mind and listen to my heart.[4]

Jack Lowe:

For 20 years I have run every morning with two other guys. I spend time listening and openly sharing.[5]

Jim Balkcom:

I jog and talk out loud to my creator. I've gotten answers to and made the most significant decisions in my life that way. Without fail a path will come to me.[6]

Bruce Bertell:

Reflection is a constant part of my life…I use a mindfulness meditation.[7]

Tessa Martinez Pollack:

There's a place I can go into in myself where I can recover balance.[8]

Bob Veazie:

Dialogue is the way I reflect. Dialogue leads to a space that is sacred. When I go into that space with people at work and there is a heart-level listening…people grow, I grow. I learn from inside myself.[9]

Meg Wheatley:

If I don't start my day with peace I won't find it out there. I've been meditating for twelve years. I've seen hard times evaporate if I take time to pause, and a different kind of intelligence comes through.[10]

Reflective practices can take many forms: walks, meditations, dream work, journaling, dialogue, and coaching partnerships—whatever centers you on what matters most. Greenleaf's archived journals show that he asked himself, *What is my capacity for greatness?*[11] The writings in his journal tell us that as he reflected on this question he realized that his capacity for greatness would not materialize until he put in check concern with possessions, and until he stopped burying himself in his work. He obviously acted on these insights, and the servant-leadership movement was born.

Reflecting from the Heart—One Person at a Time

> It is not important that you write books, achieve high status, etc. It is important that the quality of your life be extraordinary, and that you carry this quality into the work of the world.[12]
>
> —Robert Greenleaf

Servant-leaders are speaking more and more frequently about love and caring in the workplace. At TDIndustries, CEO Jack Lowe reminds us, "caring, trusting relationships got us through our organization's toughest time in 1989, and allowed us to celebrate our 50th anniversary this year as one of the 100 best Companies to Work for in America."

Many times the development of trust and caring happens one person at a time. Consider Jim Balkcom's story about creating a high-trust culture among 420 employees as CEO of Techsonic Industries.

> If you can get a message to the people working around you that you really care about them, and that care is something you will put into action, you form a bond that transcends duty. But, you can't fool anybody. If you don't develop a trusting relationship you have nothing. But if you don't have it in your heart, it just doesn't work. You can't fake trust. People just see right through you. You have to go to your heart and reflect from that place. This is not only a good thing to do—it is also ultimately the most profitable way of doing business.
>
> The toughest decision for me as a leader is to deal with an individual who has helped get this company to where it is today, maybe someone who has made a major contribution in the past, but for some reason things aren't

working now. You have to be candid. It's unfair to do anything else.

Jim points out that it is not going to be simple or easy to reflect from your heart when you're making your toughest decisions. There are a lot of misconceptions about heart wisdom. Using heart wisdom does not mean being a pushover.

As a trusting servant-leader you will be hurt and disappointed. You will make yourself vulnerable. You will open yourself up. And there are people who will try to step all over that. You will be disappointed, hurt, shocked, and if you're not careful, you could become cynical. The way I deal with this is I do it wide open, in front of God and the whole world. I don't hide any of it.[13]

For example, one time we'd had dramatic growth, from 10 million to 60 million dollars in two or three years. We grew from 100 people [employees] to 250 people. A lot of people were not aligned with the mission and culture. As I was reading a suggestion out of the suggestion box that month there was an attack on me. My intentions were being called into question. I always read cold turkey from the suggestion box so I continued even though the attack seemed vicious and hurtful. I continued to read and gave my response even though my voice cracked.[14]

Jim had to work through many of these kinds of experiences as the company continued to grow and succeed dramatically.

Everybody at Techsonic Industries has seen me laugh, sob, get really mad, etc. And they eventually come to know my feelings are genuine. My director of human resources used to come into my office in despair. She would say "these people just don't appreciate what we give to them." She'd throw her head in her hands in frustration. My continual retort would be, "Deborah, our goal is to win one person a day, or one a month, or one a year." If we work at it long enough we will win, one by one. Something will happen in someone's life where they will be able to connect, or they'll see someone model servant-leadership behavior, or they'll see somebody close to them change. And we keep increasing the circle and increasing the circle, one by one.

I began my training for servant-leadership right at home. My father, who is still alive, is a very humble man. He went through many severe challenges, but he never lost hope. He taught me to love. I thought about how my employees cast their lot with me. They trusted me. I thought to myself, what can I do for them? My partners and I created a stock ownership plan, giving 20% of our stock to the employee ownership plan. When the stock went up from $300,000 to almost $8 million, families were able to do things never before possible. Those who didn't even have high school educations could send their kids to college. Those living in homes without running water could build new homes. The success of Techsonic was unleashing the creativity within everybody through caring, trust and love. I still talk to a lot of former Techsonic employees, and the conversation usually ends with "I love you," which is from the heart. The fact of the matter is that this is the most profitable way to do business. It drives profits. It motivates people. Success is not just making 12 cents more per share this quarter.[15]

Enhancing Reflective Capacities through Coaching

You need not be a "professional coach" to benefit from using coaching for enhancing reflective capacities. All servant-leaders serve as coaches at times, even though many times, it goes unnoticed, or opportunities are missed. When you do performance reviews, when you spend time one-on-one with people, when you brainstorm how to get out of a crisis-management mode or a repetitive pattern of dysfunction in the organization, there is an opportunity for coaching. Old ideas about coaching are drawn from the view that coaching is advice given in order to get "buy-in" or show another the way to go. But Greenleaf calls us to the task of serving others so they may become more discerning, more capable, and more responsible.

Excellent coaches achieve that high standard by helping people focus on their own visions and relationships, their own hearts. This kind of coaching is all about accessing inner wisdom, not giving outer direction. It's about staying in the tension each of us experiences when we hold on to great dreams. When servant-leaders are suspended between a vision for what is possible and what they are experiencing in their current reality, there is a tendency to either deny current reality or give up the dream. Great coaching helps one to stay in the tension, and from there to access different ways or qualities of knowing. One such quality is "heart wisdom."

Listening to Your Heart Wisdom

> We now have scientific evidence that the heart sends us
> emotional and intuitive signals....Within each of us
> there exists an organizing and central intelligence that
> can lift us beyond our problems and into a new
> experience of fulfillment even in the midst of chaos.[16]
> —Childre and Martin

To access your own heart wisdom, attend to three practices: silence, wondering, and listening deeply to your heart.

1. Silence

It starts with silence. Hearing what lies very deep always starts with silence. Buckminster Fuller intentionally did not talk for two entire years, and after that developed the geodesic dome and did some of his most creative thinking. Gregg Levoy, in his book, *Callings: Finding and Following an Authentic Life*, tells us that at the times he makes his toughest decisions he needs to go to a place of silence, and *"hold that silence up to my ears like an empty shell, and listen to the roar of my own life....We are after some-*

thing that lies beneath all that noise...that is literally un-think-able....A penetrating quiet inside."[17]

Every time I begin a coaching session, I ask for a moment of silence. Although clients may at first see this as odd, it soon becomes a vital part of each session for both of us. Silence is such a simple thing, and yet, the quality of the conversation is exponentially enriched by taking that time.

2. Wondering

Be willing to wonder and ask open questions. This will get you into a reflective place much more quickly. Some of our most creative geniuses have spent a lot of time in wonderment and silence. Einstein, like many others, was known for his openness to wonder.

In order to ask open questions I start with the words, "I wonder if...." This helps me remember that I am not giving advice or trying to lead the conversation. My intention is simply to explore. I have learned that leading others in a specific direction won't help them discover their own wisdom, gifts, passion, and creativity. You know you're tapping into wonderment if people become more open, more enlarged, as you speak with them, rather than shrink down due to feeling put on the spot or grilled.

3. Listening to Heart Wisdom

Greenleaf tells us that we must use foresight for great leadership. But how do you develop the greatest foresight? Greenleaf left a lot of time in his life for open spaces, wondering, and reflection. He explained, "I did not get the notion of the 'servant as leader' from conscious logic. Rather it came to me as an intuitive insight."[18]

Heart wisdom is the wisdom that we all have inside when we slow down, cut out the external noise, and listen to that place in us that is connected to our soul.

Access to the intuitive often comes through an expanded peacefulness and an expanded heart. Chilean biologist Humberto

Maturana tells us that love expands intelligence. That when we are truly seen in the legitimacy of who we are—in true relationship—greater coherence and intelligence occur. It arises in true relationship. Rigid behavior, angry emotions, withholding love keep us stuck. Have you ever found that a change of heart changes the way you think? A change from negative competition to a collaborative spirit of caring can actually increase intelligence. As Maturana says, "Love is the only emotion that expands intelligence."[19]

The Heartmath Institute conducts research on accessing heart wisdom, and there are other initiatives like Parker Palmer's work with clearness committees. References for those approaches are included at the end of the essay and they are highly recommended. The purpose of this essay is to offer a few guiding ideas, examples of coaching from heart wisdom, and to share a few stories. For now, let's rejoin Virginia Duncan Gilmore as she reflects further on that initial call from her heart described earlier and how coaching has sustained it.

Virginia did some reflecting on the history of women in her family. Many who went before her were creative, relationship-oriented women with great imagination. Yet, they died, never having a chance to fully develop their calls:

> I knew my life had to be different. I felt a deep yearning to leave the family business so I could focus on what I cared about the most. I began to hold a vision in which the business was sold and I could go out in the world with choice to live my passion and purpose. Within six months, the vision found form.

The market changed and the family business moved into a position to be sold. Still, letting go did not occur without some pain. Virginia was led to face issues of changing or ending:

> I heard a calling to go out into nature to a beautiful area in northern Wisconsin, Door County, for healing and reflection. It was as if my heart was cracking open into something greater. The image that came to me to help me let go

108

was to let go with an energy as vibrant as the color of the beautiful Fall leaves. When I returned I was able to do all the things that would add value as I exited the company.

By accessing the wisdom of her heart, Virginia eventually reached her hope for financial independence and moved into a new call of philanthropy:

I always believed I would share the financial resources from the company in ways to make a difference.

Virginia recently formed a foundation, the Sophia Foundation, as an affiliate with her local community foundation. Her two children and other affiliates serve on the board of directors with her as she continues to guide her strategic philanthropic direction to support the human journey toward wisdom and wholeness. She continues to listen even more carefully to the wisdom of her heart. One way she does this is through our coaching partnership:

In relationship with Deborah, my coaching partner of seven years, I more deeply experience spirit's call and I look for the flow. If the flow is not there I am learning not to take it personally. I make decisions differently than I did before. I wait. I journal. I seek out that place of knowing…then I act. If I can be present and available in the heart space, I connect with a different knowing. This is the foundation upon which I build my work now.

I believe that each of us has an inner wisdom that is of the nature to best guide our souls. The wisdom in coaching partnership expands within each of us. The challenge is to create enough space within me—within you, within us—the deep listening capacity to hear the heart's call. In the coaching relationship Virginia asks herself, "How is my heart?" Just receiving the question and being heard is an incredible gift. It is asking how are YOU in relationship to what you LOVE?

Beyond all the focus on outer results and the mechanics involved in getting work done, Virginia hears her call more clearly through the space of exploration that arises in the coaching relationship.

Coaching for Heart Wisdom

> Some day, after we have mastered the winds, the waves, the tides, and gravity, we will harness for God the energies of love; and then for the second time in the history of the world we will have discovered fire![20]
>
> —Teilhard de Chardin

Opening our hearts and listening can be a challenge at those times when it is needed the most. Here is a process that you may find useful if you come upon a situation in which you, or someone you are serving, is feeling stuck.

1. Begin by thinking of a wisdom figure, someone in your life who loves you and has guided you in a loving way, or someone whose ideas you love from a book you read, or a grandparent. Take some time now to think of someone loving and wise.
2. Relax and take a moment of silence. In the silence I clear the decks of cluttered ideas. I feel my body relax.
3. Describe the challenge in your life. I have to decide whether to take on a contract that will require a great deal of sacrifice for me. There is no easy answer to this question.
4. Notice the ideas that come to you about the challenge. If I take on this project it will require sacrifice, and it is a huge financial risk. I'm asking myself, is this really the right thing to do? Or, is this my foolish pride? Is this my ego leading me into something, or am I truly serving a higher purpose here? Why do I feel so called to continue?
5. Pause in silence. Think slowly and un-layer from all the things you thought were so important.
   I start with silence and stillness. I let go of all the things around me...the inner critical voice and mon-

key-mind chatter, etc., so that I can hear what my heart has to say. I make myself just a little willing to walk through whatever fear may arise.

6. Move your attention to your heart. As I imagine the presence of my grandmother who always offered me love, my heart lights up. I also think of my ninety-two-year-old mentor, Edith. It takes me to a place in my heart. I silently think about how much love I feel in her presence. I feel my heart open.

7. Ask yourself an open question, "I wonder if...." I ask myself the question, "I wonder...is this the right thing to do to take on this contract and risk at this time?"

8. Listen to hear your heart's answer. I feel the calm inside. I begin to get a sense of intelligent love that says "yes." I may picture my grandmother or my mentor Edith speaking or hear a quiet answer inside. I hear "yes." Yes, even though it's been hard this is the right thing. Here is some guidance on how to do this. Don't push so much. The more you push, the less things will happen. This project requires greater support. Don't take this on in a halfhearted manner. Take this project on wholeheartedly. But do so in very small steps with much more support than you had planned. Then this will indeed be a life giving, successful endeavor that will help you and many others.

9. Journal your heart's response and further reflections. As I listen, it is almost as if there is a cloud lifted around me. I feel energy, excitement, and an inner congruence. Can I trust what I heard? As I decide to trust, I have a new confidence about how to approach things. I then begin to think about how to move forward. It will take some difficult conversations to move this forward, but when I am so clear in my heart, it is not difficult to say these things.

This exercise takes time and silence. You will know you're on track if you feel calm and peaceful, if you hear—or *feel*—a quieter voice inside. It is a quality of being that resonates with your heart.

From that new place, you think of a new response to the issue. Sometimes something will strike you as if you remember something you had forgotten, or like a camera lens that is focused so that what was fuzzy suddenly becomes clear as day. Other times peacefulness will lead to an answer that comes later in the day.

Taking Action

A qualification for leadership is that one can tolerate a sustained wide span of awareness so that one better "sees it as it is."[21]

—Robert K. Greenleaf

Coaching, whether for yourself or another person, is a way to expand wisdom, deepen relationship, and implement servant-leadership in your organization and your life. The next time you are confronted with a difficult decision about your work—an important employee relationship, succession planning, training, or severance—think of it as a coachable moment. Stop and take a moment to reflect on how you might achieve greater clarity about the situation and, therefore, a better decision. A moment for reflection may be one of the most important actions you take in the day. You'll find that with the smallest amount of effort you can accomplish a great deal. Seek out opportunities to create coaching partnerships.

Chapter Six

HOLISTIC SERVANT-LEADERSHIP: A MULTIDIMENSIONAL APPROACH

George SanFacon and Larry C. Spears

This article was made possible by our dear friend and mentor, Curtis E. (Bill) Bottum, who was an avid follower and friend of Robert K. Greenleaf. As president and CEO of Townsend and Bottum, a worldwide leader in power plant construction, Bill advanced servant-leadership as the company's guiding philosophy and established the first council of equals there. He also served on the Greenleaf Center's board of trustees for over twenty years. We each spent a lot of time with Bill, both separately and together, discussing servant-leadership and the first-among-equals governance model. This article is, in part, an extension of those discussions and that experience. As such, it is dedicated to Bill's wonderful and enduring spirit.

Introduction

Robert K. Greenleaf first published his seminal essays, *The Servant as Leader* and *The Institution as Servant*, in the early 1970s. In them, he promoted his hopeful vision of a better society, one more just and more loving with greater opportunities for all. He claimed that achieving this was possible by improving the performance of both our leaders and our institutions. Over the subsequent decades, an increasing number of people around the world have been studying these essays and other Greenleaf writings, and striving to live out the ideals and principles of what is now called, "servant-leadership." This writing provides a practical framework and multidimensional map for those so engaged. As such, it is meant to:

1. Identify and integrate the *generic* aspects of servant-leadership, those common to most enterprises (including business and private enterprise, not-for-profits, health care, education, and government);
2. Provide insight into how those aspects or dimensions not only differ from one another but also relate to one another, ultimately comprising an integrated whole;
3. Support practitioners in their work and journey from intention through practical application; and,
4. Encourage the continuing evolution and growth of the servant-leadership movement in an ever-changing and ever-challenging world.

In developing and writing this essay, we have tried to remain true to the core teachings of Greenleaf while including related insights from our own experience. In addition, we have reframed and expanded concepts and language to update and better place this work within the context of today's realities and emerging worldviews.

The Potential and Paradox of Servant-Leadership

Robert Greenleaf had remarkable wisdom and insight about things that really matter. Decades ago, when most conventional leaders focused primarily on furthering the goals of a privileged few, he challenged them to also consider the needs of others and the less privileged. He claimed that a good, just, and desirable society depends upon leaders who *care;* that is, leaders who extend consideration to all those affected by the enterprise. These *stakeholders* include employees, local communities, other "tribes" and peoples, living systems, and future generations. Greenleaf thereby presaged the most significant issue that confronts our increasingly interdependent world, recently framed as follows by Sharif Abdullah:

> In a world of six billion humans and countless other beings, how can we create circumstances wherein each can flourish, without limiting the life expression of others? In short, how can we create a world that truly works for all?[1]

This is the underlying dilemma and challenge in Greenleaf's work for our leaders, our institutions, and ourselves.

Greenleaf spent over half a century working in the fields of management research, development, and education, trying to improve the performance of both for-profit and non-profit institutions. As a lifelong student and participant in how things get done in organizations, he distilled his observations in a series of essays and books centered on the themes of *caring* and "The Servant as Leader." Throughout these writings, he discussed the need for a better approach to leadership—one that puts serving others first. Greenleaf urged those in formal leadership positions to ask themselves two questions: "Whom do you serve?" and "For what purpose?" He also urged leaders to take a more holistic approach to work, promote a sense of community, and to share power in decision making. Through his writings and work, Greenleaf sought to stimulate thought and action for building a better society.

It is worth noting that the words *servant* and *leader* are usually thought of as opposites—and when two opposites are brought together in a creative and meaningful way, a paradox emerges. At first glance, the paradox seems contradictory or opposed to common sense, but there is also an underlying sense that it could be true. The overall effect is to wake us up to new possibilities, ones that transcend previous ways of thinking and believing. So who is this paradoxical servant-leader? Anyone dedicated to serving others who then chooses to formally lead in some way. According to Greenleaf:

> It begins with the natural feeling that one wants to serve, to serve first. Then conscious choice brings one to aspire to lead. The difference manifests itself in the care taken by the servant—first to make sure that other people's highest priority needs are being served. The best test is: Do those served grow as persons; do they, while being served, become healthier, wiser, freer, more autonomous, more likely themselves to become servants? And, what is the effect on the least privileged in society? Will they benefit or at least not be further deprived?[2]

Many positional leaders have concluded that servant-leadership is the right thing to do, and subsequently decide to embrace it. This has been an important way through which servant-leadership has grown and been advanced over the years. However, Greenleaf titled his essay, *The Servant as Leader* not *The Leader as Servant*. He thereby called upon people who are "natural servants" to actively participate in leading organizations and institutions on behalf of the common good. He specifically asked those who have a vocation for service to then consciously seek and fill positions as leaders dedicated to creating a more caring society. At its core, servant-leadership is a long-term, transformational approach to life and work—a way of being—that has great potential for creating positive, nonviolent change throughout our society and the world.

Motives, Means, and Ends—The Ethical Dimensions of Leadership

How does one proceed from intention to practice as a servant-leader? Greenleaf left a clue in the name he first used for the fledgling, nonprofit organization he founded in 1964, the Center for Applied Ethics. Evidently, in some way or at some level, he viewed *ethics*, or *moral reasoning*, as a compass or pathway for

116

effective leadership and a better world. According to ethicists, sound moral reasoning requires a holistic approach—that is an appraisal of three distinct dimensions: motives, means, and ends.[3] *Motives* are about intentions; "why" we do something. *Means* are about methods; "how" we do it. And *ends* are about outcomes; "what" we are trying to accomplish. Ethics demands that each of these be judged as right, good, and desirable by both those involved and those affected. Separately appraising each of these dimensions of servant-leadership—motives, means, and ends— can help clarify both philosophy and practice. It can also lead to insights about how these dimensions relate to one another, as well as the specific work that servant-leaders are called to do and live out in each domain.

Motives and Intentions

As we grow into personhood, we become increasingly concerned about others. This is how human development generally proceeds. Each higher stage of this development does not mean that we stop caring for ourselves, but that we include more and more others for whom we also evidence a genuine consideration and concern.[4] We thereby become increasingly committed to enlarging the lives of others. Whether we are following or leading, our intention is to serve—to extend what we want for our loved ones and ourselves to all. This intention is the taproot of servant-leadership, and the seedbed from which the impulse arises to make a positive difference in the world. It is from this interior place that real change happens, first in ourselves and then in the social systems in which we participate.

In this dimension, servant-leaders are called upon to *care*. Of course, we each land on a different place along this spectrum of caring, which ranges from *self* to *all*. Nevertheless, we are called to serve all—ourselves, our loved ones, our neighbors, our tribe, our people, other peoples, future generations, other life forms, living systems, and even creation itself. At the most basic level, our development is about growing into this expanded embrace. Somewhere along the journey, even though we have been enjoying comfort and material gain under the established order, we become willing to change that order to further a world that works for all. This makes deep, nonviolent change truly possible. One pioneering teacher put it this way:

> [These] individuals...tend to develop a sense of planetary citizenship, reverence for life in all its forms, deep ecological sensitivity, spirituality of a universal and all-encompassing type, aversion to violence, and reluctance to view aggression as an acceptable form of conflict resolution. Such radical inner transformation and rise to a new level of consciousness might be humanity's only real chance for survival.[5]

Means and Methods

While motives and intentions relate to the source of our energy for taking action, means and methods relate to how that energy expresses itself in the world. We can divide these expressions into two major categories: (1) ways of being, and (2) institutional systems. The former relates to the leader as an individual; the latter relates to the organizational frameworks and infrastructure used by the leader.

Servant-Leader Ways of Being, Capacities, and Roles. There are ways of being and capacities that are central to how servant-leaders develop and engage in the world. These include, but are not limited to: awareness, presence, availability, reflection, empathy, listening and receptivity, acceptance of others, intuition, generosity, foresight, and transparency. With these and other qualities available as reliable resources, servant-leaders are able to fulfill key roles—as stewards, role models, healers, change agents, and community-builders—in creating better enterprises and a better world.

Institutional Systems and Governance. Conventional thinking assumes that we just need to get the right people into the right positions for things to get better. But that is only partly true; while we *do* need good, competent people serving as leaders, we *also* need effective institutional and organizational systems. That is because systems are powerful containers for the human experience; they shape the life that is poured into them. But only formal leaders are officially sanctioned to change the system. To paraphrase one management guru, "Workers work *in* systems, leaders work *on* systems."[6] Greenleaf identified the system of *organization*, what he referred to as "people and structure," as fundamental to better leadership and a better society.[7] Structure relates to how power, rights, and responsibilities are distributed, which encompasses the executive functions. It is, therefore, the *metasystem* for the enterprise, through which all other systems are controlled and mediated. Here, Greenleaf advocated partnership rather than domination, admonishing leaders to be "first among equals" on teams of equals (another Greenleaf paradox), rather than "lone chiefs" or bosses atop hierarchical pyramids.[8]

Besides working on themselves, effective servant-leaders work on their institutional and organizational systems. In this dimension, the two-fold process of transformation—self and system—is the calling of servant-leadership.

Ends and Outcomes

A World that Works for All—this is the ultimate goal of the servant-leadership movement. But there is a long way to go. While current social and economic systems have brought unparalleled wealth to some people, they have also brought marginalization and misery to many. At the global level, the benefits of economic growth have become increasingly concentrated—the richest 20 percent of people in the world consume 86 percent of everything produced, while the poorest 20 percent are pressed into absolute poverty, barely surviving in urban slums or depressed rural areas.[9] At the local level, our organizations and enterprises are dominated by lone-chief (boss/subordinate) structures, and jobs that are smaller than the people occupying them. Such conditions fuel resentment, division, and conflict. To make matters worse, our consumer-based culture and lifestyles are resulting in the overexploitation and destruction of nature and living systems. All of this is being compounded by the negative, unintended consequences of technology (including nuclear proliferation and global warming), which potentially threatens all life on the planet.

The fact is: our contemporary world is socially, politically, and ecologically unsustainable. As recently noted:

> We cannot remain as we are, nor can we go back to conditions that are behind us. We can only move forward, but not on the same path we have been following. We need to find a new direction.[10]

Servant-leadership is part of this new direction, which entails striking a better balance between self-interest and the common good. In this dimension, servant-leaders are called to lead their enterprises in:

Transitioning to goods and services that promote a workable and meaningful world;

Embracing a *Triple Bottom Line*—sustaining people, profits, and the planet; and,

Adopting the practice of *moral symmetry*—balancing the legitimate needs of all those affected by the enterprise.

A Chart of Servant-Leadership

The following chart, *Dimensions of Servant-Leadership*, provides an overview of these domains and their relationship to one another.

THE DIMENSIONS OF SERVANT-LEADERSHIP		
Dimensions	**Basic Concepts and Goals**	**The Calling for Servant-Leaders**
Motives and Intentions **The "Why?"**	"It begins with the natural feeling that one wants to serve."[11] Personal aspirations for leadership come from a basic desire to enlarge the lives of others, rather than a desire and drive for more power, recognition or material gain.	Develop and grow the personal capacity (depth and range) to *care*. Develop an expanded embrace that extends to everyone affected by the enterprise.

Dimensions	Basic Concepts and Goals	The Calling for Servant-Leaders
Means and Methods **The "How?"**	**I. The Servant-Leader—Ways of Being, Capacities and Roles**	
	A better world can be built by better people. There are ways of being, capacities and roles that embody servant-leadership, both representing its expression and furthering its realization in the world. These can be learned and deepened through practice.	Increase personal capacities for: awareness, presence, availability, reflection, empathy, listening and receptivity, acceptance of others, intuition, generosity, foresight, simplicity and transparency. Fulfill organizational roles of: steward, role model, healer, change agent, and community builder.
	II. The System—Organization and Governance	
	Institutional and organizational systems are people-building and life-giving, rather than people-using and spirit-killing. Power is shared. Leaders are "first among equals" on teams of equals, rather than "lone chiefs" atop hierarchical pyramids.[12]	Transition to a shared governance model that incorporates the *first among equals* concept. Use participatory approaches to workplace issues and practice. Implement new-paradigm approaches, such as "open book" management, gainsharing, employee stock ownership programs (ESOPs) and self-directed teams (SDTs).
Ends and Outcomes **The "What?"**	Those affected by the servant-leader and the enterprise have the experience of being served in a way that builds a society "that is more just and loving...with greater opportunities for all." Systems and institutions are socially, politically, and environmentally sustainable. The world works for all. Every person has the opportunity to discover and live out who they are and can be.	Transition to goods and services that promote a workable and meaningful world. Embrace a *Triple Bottom Line* for the enterprise—promoting social equity, delivering profits and sustaining the planet. Practice *moral symmetry*—balancing the legitimate needs of all those affected by the enterprise.

Reality—A Seamless Whole

While the boundary lines we impose on reality can be helpful in understanding it, there is, nevertheless, an underlying oneness at work. So even though we divide servant-leadership into separate dimensions—motives, means, and ends—it actually works as a seamless whole. These parts, therefore, need to be reassembled into the single reality that actually exists. We can do this by simply recognizing that shortfalls in any specific aspect or domain will ultimately limit progress and outcomes in other parts, as well as the whole. The point is: the various aspects and dimensions of servant-leadership function most effectively as an integrated whole.

The Journey

The challenge for us as servant-leaders is to actually live out the underlying ideals and better realize them in the world. The question is: How do we, as servant-leaders, hold our organizations and ourselves accountable for what we are trying to live out?

One way is to make periodic assessments, taking inventory of both our systems and ourselves. Through honest reflection and feedback (most importantly, to-and-from those being affected), we can learn where things stand on a range of possibilities for each characteristic and dimension. We can then redirect our efforts to achieve better outcomes. Another way is to consider the work of this moment—that is whatever is at hand and needs to be addressed—as an opportunity to live out and express the ideals. As one sage put it: "Everything we face is an opportunity to walk the path."[13] In this case, we simply do what servant-leadership calls us to do with what is in front of us right now, in this moment. Either way, we can move along the path incrementally by simply taking the next small step. And we can do this again and again, whether we are working to improve our listening skills (self) or transitioning to a first-among-equals form of governance (system). In our experience, servant-leadership is most always "a thousand-mile journey taken one small step at a time."

Summary

Effective servant-leaders consciously engage each of the dimensions of servant-leadership: (1) motives and intentions, (2) means and methods, (3) outcomes and results and seek to understand them as a gestalt. This is a holistic approach to the work. These leaders thereby create spaces where individuals and communities can heal, grow, and thrive through mutual caring and trust. Organizational life thereby is transformed gradually from a treadmill and struggle of opposing forces to a journey and celebration in co-creativity. Through this process, both natural servants and positional leaders become servant-leaders, the journey becomes the destination, and the world becomes a better place for all.

High moral values and excellence must dominate the twenty-first century if progress is to have positive meaning. Through ideas like those of Robert Greenleaf's servant-leadership, such a way of life is now well within our reach.[14]

—Bill Bottum

Chapter Seven
BEARING WITNESS: INSIGHTS FOR SERVANT-LEADERS

James A. Autry

We may not be, as some suggest, "called" to work. We may indeed just start working to make money, to improve our status, to create a future, or just to stay off the dole, as they used to say.

I was very reluctant to get a job when I was a kid. I did not want to work. It seemed inconvenient, far too wasteful of my time. But we were poor. I did a little of everything—carried the morning newspaper on a regular route, and then sold the afternoon paper on a corner to the businessmen who would stop in their cars on the way home from the office. I picked and chopped cotton on a farm, worked on a bread truck, on a construction crew, as a soda jerk, waiter, copyboy, photographer's assistant, teletype operator, musician, reporter, and photographer—all before I graduated from college. And this does not include my work scholarships as a university public relations writer, darkroom technician, and—yes, I was paid to do it—drum major of the university marching band.

Not one of those jobs did I do for anything but money. Not for training or education, not for the advancement of a career, not to create a productive future, and certainly not for personal or spiritual growth. But for money (and occasionally for the chance to be around women, but that's another story).

My mother worked in degrading low-level jobs only because she had to make money. However, I believe the reason that abil-

ity to use a comptometer machine—sort of a primitive calcula-
tor—meant so much to her was that it evidenced a skill, the mas-
tery of something almost mystical that elevated her to another
plain of achievement, in her mind something like a professional.
And, of course, she credited God. She felt God had, as the old
hymn said, planted her feet on higher ground.

Her belief that God had helped her did not stop there. God
had helped her for a reason, and the reason was that she would
now be in a better position to "witness for Jesus." This, in her
view, was what we all were to do, those of us who called ourselves Christians.

"Jimmy," she would tell me, "Surely you can use your paper
route to witness for Jesus." Naturally, I thought that impossible.
What was I supposed to do, ask one of the people in the Linden
Avenue mansions or in one of the white trash shotgun houses,
"Have you accepted Jesus as your personal savior?" or "Would
you like to go to church with me?" I remember once or twice trying to summon the courage to approach the subject with one of
my customers, but I did not have Mother's confidence that the
Lord would save me from ridicule and embarrassment.

That is still my fear as I speak and write about the spirit of
work. Yet I know that the "liberation of the human spirit" in the
context of the work we choose to do—even if we choose that
work only for the money—is at the heart of the healing that must
happen between management and employees if we are to save
American business from a debilitating and destructive crisis of
trust in the wake of all the downsizing of the past several years.

No, it's not the same as witnessing for Jesus, yet I do believe
that our work gives us one of our best opportunities to look for
the best—the Divine—in others and to manifest the best—the
Divine—in ourselves. Indeed, I believe any good work we do for
or with others is also God's work.

Just what is good work with others? It is any work, no matter how routine or menial, done with generosity, positive intention, a spirit of community, and a commitment to doing it well.

What is good work done for others? It is anything done with
unselfishness and generosity, a putting aside (or overcoming) of
ego, for the benefit of another person. But what if that other per-

son is a jerk, a bad person, who doesn't give a damn for you or your good work? So much more the need for the courage I could not muster as paperboy and so much more the reason to try.

As Lao-tzu asks in the *Tao Te Ching*, "What is a good man but a bad man's teacher? What is a bad man but a good man's job?"[1]

In previous books, I have described my skepticism of companies that make much public hoo-ha about their claims to conduct their business according to Christian principles, then use those principles to try to prescribe and control behavior, and to repress their employees rather than to liberate and ennoble them.

Yet I know of—and respect—business executives who do use their religious principles to guide them in liberating the human spirit and to bring dignity and legitimate power to their employees. I believe this is true of such American business leaders as Max DePree, author and former CEO of Herman Miller, Inc., his successor, Kermit Campbell, Peter and Jack Herschend of Silver Dollar City, Irv Hockaday of Hallmark, Mike Moody of AT&T, among others.

Still, there is a certain uneasiness, a certain risk, in this whole subject. Some of the risk is put to rest, I believe, by concentrating on the spirit in work, the opportunity it gives us to find personal and spiritual growth, rather than focusing on a particular sectarian interpretation of that spirituality.

But what does it mean, "spiritual growth?" I don't have a simple answer, and perhaps not even a good answer, but I believe spiritual growth has a lot to do with opportunities we have to connect on a deeper level with one another. I want to believe that we find easy connection through our shared joys, but I know in my heart that the connections come most readily from shared loss and pain, and that is because in times of pain there is usually nothing to say to one another except the obvious, which, I believe, leaves us searching for other expressions. Those expressions, if indeed we are open to the opportunities, may make appropriate the things we usually find difficult—a touch, even a hug, tears, a long walk, a note with a poem enclosed, and the assurance that we will be thinking about our colleague or friend, or praying for them.

Much trivia drops away when someone says, "I have cancer,"

or when someone's child is seriously ill, or when a loved one dies. The only thing to do in those circumstances is show that you care.

I used to question the value of sympathy notes and flowers, but when my mother died, the first death of an immediate family member, I remember walking into that funeral home in Ripley, Mississippi, and being overwhelmed by the flowers from friends and co-workers. The same when my father died and, six months later, my brother. The affection I felt expressed by the flowers and by the notes, as simple and obvious as those words were, was a revelation to me, and it awakened a recognition of connection that far transcended my previously held assessments of those relationships, professional and personal. In that recognition I believe I experienced some inkling of the spiritual possibilities within our everyday relationships.

This is not to say that those possibilities come only at times of pain. There simply is no denying something ineffable just in the very act of working together and in accomplishing together what we set out to accomplish. I believe we feel this something but often don't recognize it much less understand how to express it. We can't even put labels on it. We say we "love" our jobs, we find them "challenging and rewarding," we are "motivated," we are "team players," we take "pride" in what we do.

Managers talk about "vision," "excellence," "quality," and "empowerment." We coach and are coached; we mentor and are mentored. We seek continuous improvement. We want always to be learning. We talk about ethics and integrity, about health and healing. We use all of this language, but what does it literally say about that ineffable something we feel about what we have chosen to do? Very little. The same is true as we try to express those feelings through parties and celebrations and conferences, through pep rallies and retreats, through the simple act of an informal get-together after work.

But those who are willing to take a more metaphorical view will find that these superficial words and activities symbolize the most profound expressions of our deepest selves, and will understand that we simply have not developed an adequate vocabulary for what we feel as we seek meaning, dignity, and growth in the everydayness of our work and lives.

Among my regrets as a manager is that I did not develop a clear enough sense of this metaphorical view in earlier years, and when I did, that I did not do more to help my colleagues and employees find that meaning.

Certainly, I had no understanding about this as a young man, but I recognize now that several profound things were trying to make their way through in those years. One was a sense of worth and esteem I began to feel as a copyboy for the Associated Press. I would pronounce "The Associated Press" with an air of great importance, much the way Mother pronounced "comptometer." Later, I came to say "AP" as if every boy in my high school should know what those initials stood for.

The sheer size of the organization, its dominant place in the world of news gathering, the energy of the office—reporters shouting, photographers rushing still-wet photographs from the dark room, the noise of the machines and the absolute miracle of them—and my place as a cog in this great wheel gave me feelings I had never had. Never. I was no longer a kid who had few clothes, little money, no car, and no time to play sports because he had to work. I was "with" the Associated Press, and the Associated Press needed what I could do.

Another dim understanding came in those moments when all of us—reporters, photographers, teletype operators, and I—had worked together and had beaten the United Press with a story. We would stand at the teletype machine, watching it run as Harrell Alien or one of the expert teletype operators punched the tape, fed it into the transmitter, then with consummate skill punched the story fast enough to keep up—and even gain on— the tape as it clicked through the feeder, sending it signals that appeared magically on the machine. It was a particular spirit of celebration if our story ran on the "A" wire, the national news wire of the AP. I could not have used the words then or under- stood the concept they represent, but I was participating in the community of work and feeling the spirit of it.

The community was made even more real at Christmas, when on Christmas Eve the various AP bureaus around the country sent elaborate Christmas greetings over the mostly idle machines. There wasn't much news to transmit, so the artists of the teletype were given the opportunity to exhibit their best work.

On my first Christmas, Harrell Alien asked, "Would you like to send your own Christmas greetings over the state wire?" I was overwhelmed. I was taking typing in high school in hopes of becoming a teletype operator but had never used the machines. Harrell set it up, and I carefully punched Xs into a simple pyramid design of a Christmas tree, and wrote, "Merry Christmas to all Tennessee AP staffers." I loved using words like *staffer*.

"How shall I sign it, Harrell? Memphis Bureau?"

"Just use your own initials, 'JA/MX.'"

I put the tape on the transmitter, then hit the toggle switch and watched the state wire come to life and print my message. I tore it from the machine, a two-inch strip of low-grade paper, took it home to show my mother, then kept it in a scrapbook for years. I realize now it was more than a memento.

I would not have said "more than a memento" in those days, however. For all the good feelings I was able to have in that clattering, carbon-smudged teletype room, it was to my mind still just a place I went to work to make some money, and making money—not the human spirit, not the enrichment of the inner life, not grace—was still how I identified the meaning of my work life.

The Air Force seemed so different that I assumed there could be no connection between life as a fighter pilot and a civilian working in an office. The camaraderie, the identity, the special bonds of risk and death surely could not be replicated in some damned office building while wearing a suit and tie.

Of course, I questioned why some pilots were killed and I wasn't, but the notion it might have something to do with "grace" never entered my consciousness. A part of all pilots wants to believe that we could handle any situation and would not have been killed as others were. But that was not true. We talked a lot about luck, but I found myself doing a lot more praying in those years, traditional praying in which we bring our wish list for consideration. I think I would now classify that as being scared back into religion, and I don't think it qualifies as enlightenment.

Back in civilian life, I became immersed in work—it took me a long time to realize that it was not unlike the fighter squadron after all—but to me it was still just a job. I've often wondered why it took so long to "get it," to realize what was really going on as my friends and colleagues and I turned to and busted our asses to do good work together, to get good results, to make our boss look good to his boss.

It was not until the early eighties, when I was a senior corporate executive, that I began to understand the power of the spirit in work, the need for community and connection among workers, the opportunity for growth of many kinds that work provides. Perhaps it was the influence of friends who began to lead me on more spiritual personal paths, perhaps it was the trauma of life in those days—divorce, sickness, death—perhaps it was the fabled midlife crisis, perhaps it was as simple as being brought face-to-face with my own mortality. Whatever the reasons, I began to feel that the only choice in work and life is to find the balance and, in turn, to help others find that balance.

I began to understand the need to find meaning in the everyday things, to see the divine in others, to discover holiness in the most mundane of activities. I realized that "burn out" is not a matter of working too hard; it is a matter of finding no meaning in what we do. Not a problem of mental/physical energy but a problem of emotional energy. Not a crisis of time but a crisis of spirit. More and more I knew that what most of us need is not a getting away from the drudgery of work but a getting into the joy of work, not a separation of life and work but an integration of life and work.

To quote Rabindranath Tagore:

I slept and dreamt that life was Joy;
and then I awoke and realized
that life was Duty.
And then I went to work—and, lo
and behold I discovered that
Duty can be Joy.[2]

These understandings or realizations or moments of truth prescribed for me a path that was quite different from the one most often used in business, particularly by senior corporate executives. It was a path of leader not as boss but as servant.

Again, I found myself needing to come up with the courage to witness, and somehow it seemed more important than ever. Once I began, I found many fellow travelers. Along the way, I discovered Robert Greenleaf's writings and became familiar with the work of the Greenleaf Center for Servant-Leadership.

I found that virtually everything I had learned from my newsboy days through the Air Force days and into senior management pointed incontrovertibly in the same direction: toward the inside, toward the inner life, toward the ineffable.

There are many lessons about the spirit of work, and three of the most important are these: we should be thankful for work itself; we should be thankful for the people we work with; and we should recognize and be thankful for the grace of our spiritual possibilities at work.

Six Uncomplicated Guidelines for Servant-Leaders

1. *Manage for the best and not the worst.* Focus on the good behaviors and good performance of the majority of your people, and work to affirm them. Don't concentrate, as most managers do, on the few people who do not want to do well and who can't accept trust. These people will make themselves known in good time, and you'll have ample opportunity to help them change or help them leave. In the meantime, for the sake of your good people and the atmosphere of your workplace, emphasize affirmation not prohibition.
2. *Don't engage in police work.* Also called "in-box management," this style is defined as sitting at your desk, monitoring the in-box, and waiting for someone to make a mistake so you'll have something to do. This is policing. It is NOT leading.
3. *Be honest.* Honesty is the single most important attribute in a leader's relationship with employees and fel-

low workers. Of course, honesty is difficult, but dishonesty is weakness.

4. *Trust everyone.* This is even more difficult than honesty; in fact, trust is the most difficult thing of all, because most of us are conditioned to be always checking our backsides. Remember, most people want to do a good job and will do a good job if trusted to do a good job, so don't manage for the few who don't want to do a good job. Also understand that trust in and of itself provides an inner discipline for people; also, an environment of trust creates a medium in which peer pressure provides discipline for those who have difficulty accepting trust.

5. *Let your first response also be the caring response.* Regardless of whatever management situation presents itself, always ask yourself what the most caring response would be. There'll be plenty of time for technical, professional, or functional responses after you've demonstrated that you care. And if you don't care for people, you'll never be a servant-leader and you should probably get out of management before it's too late. Save yourself a heart attack. Save your fellow workers the grief of having to deal with you. Remember the old maxim: "People want to know how much you care before they care how much you know."

6. *Care about yourself too.* The servant-leader never neglects the self, because good leadership involves caring about yourself, physically, psychologically, emotionally, and spiritually. You simply can't jumpstart other people unless your own battery is charged up.

Rules to Live and Lead By

1. *All growth and most good things come from paying attention.* This means paying attention, and attending, to the relationships in our lives, whether with a spouse or child or friend or colleague or vendor or customer.

Remember, the most important things are not obvious to the eye.

2. *Use every experience.* Every experience is connected to every other experience, from childhood throughout our lives. Everything counts—every event, every episode, every interaction. This attitude requires you to be conscious of every moment and to put your full energy into living that moment and filling it with as much meaning as possible. Too many people are so focused on getting to the next thing that they never fully embrace the thing they're doing right now.

3. *Never think of employees as "labor," as a commodity.* This is a grave mistake and an all-too-common one, particularly in organizations that employ hourly workers. Once you begin to think of people as commodities you do three things: (1) You rob work of its meaning; (2) You rob people of their opportunities to find meaning in their work; (3) Your leadership loses its humanity.

4. *Avoid the tyranny of technocracy.* The great majority of managers ignore relationships and become technocrats, putting their energies into all the stuff that is easy to measure. Not only is this the easy way to avoid the difficult work of real leadership, but it also suppresses the human spirit at work. Remember the sign on Einstein's office wall: "Not everything that counts can be counted, and not everything that can be counted counts."

5. *Abandon the career planning traps.* The most frustrated people in the business world fall into two categories: those who did not get what they planned and those who did get what they planned.

6. *Avoid "building" a resume.* You should do the work you want to do, not the work you think will make you more "marketable." There is far less future in *doing things just to have done them* rather than *doing things just for the doing of them.*

7. *Expect the unexpected and be ready to embrace change.* Everybody talks about this, but the only way to be ready is not to burden yourself with a mass of contingency plans and quick moves. Believe me; change will not happen the way you plan it to happen. It's best to simply pay attention, expect the unexpected, and go with it until you find opportunities within the chaos that change brings.

8. *Take the work seriously but don't take yourself so seriously.* It is a great temptation for managers to believe that they ARE the business, thus whatever promotes them promotes the business. One of the greatest barriers to personal growth then becomes the desire to live up to your own hype. The danger is that you will become so focused on yourself that your people and your business suffer. Tip: If you ever hear yourself say, with exasperation, "I can't be everywhere," you're taking yourself far too seriously.

9. *Do not use long-term solutions to short-term problems.* The most obvious solution is often the one that comes back to haunt you in the long run.

10. *Never run away from anything.* Always run to something. Of course, there are often reasons to leave a situation, but often the solution to a better situation comes from confronting the problem honestly and head-on rather than just leaving it behind.

Five of the Most Useful Questions in Management:

1. *What do you think we should do? Or, what do you propose?*
Use these questions judicially. And don't sound like a pop psychotherapist. If you're asked, "What do you think we should do?" answer the question. These are good questions, however, when someone or a group has outlined a situation requiring a decision. The point is to avoid jumping right in with your own decision without asking and seeking a consensus. Chances are

the people know what the decision should be, so you should honor their thinking and their hard work by seeking their answers. As it says in the *Tao Te Ching*, "When the (leader's) work is done, the people say, 'Amazing, we did it all by ourselves.'"[3]

2. *If you were in my position, what would you do now?*

This question and question number 3 are particularly excellent questions when you are in conflict, or a situation of potential conflict, with someone—either a colleague or peer or employee. You can also offer to "swap" positions, and then assume the other's position as a role-playing exercise. This can build empathy on both sides.

3. *If I could say exactly what you'd like to hear, what would it be?*

As in question number 2, this is a very good question for conflict resolution. It may not turn out that you can say what the other wants to hear, but at least the other gets to articulate the answer as he or she would like to hear it. You can then go from that point with a clearer understanding.

4. *What do you want me to do?*

You often will be surprised that people just want you to listen, to understand, and not to DO anything.

5. *If you could project ahead to the best possible outcome, the outcome you would most like to see, what would it be or what would it look like?*

This is a great question during goal-setting, coaching, or career counseling sessions. It can also be used in conflict resolution.

Four of the Most Useful Words in the World:

I could be wrong.
Or, put another way:
You may be right.

Note: You will be amazed how these four little words—put either way—will change the entire atmosphere in a room, the progress of a discussion, or the tone of a conflict. By using them, you simply open yourself to the possibility that another viewpoint or opinion may be the most appropriate one. And you demonstrate to others your willingness to admit mistakes or uncertainty. This is more powerful than you can ever imagine. Try it.

Random Advice for the Servant-Leader:

Include employees' personal growth as a part of your planning. It can pay off in long-term productivity. When discussing performance standards, ask employees: "What are you doing to improve/develop/enjoy yourself on or off the job?"

Recognize that ego is the biggest problem in leadership. Be willing to give up "taking credit" in the short run. Instead, focus on creating the optimum environment for everybody's success. Remember: "You can accomplish anything as long as you don't care who gets the credit."

Have employees write their own performance standards and performance appraisals. Prepare your version. Then compare them. Sit down together and discuss: "What are your strengths?" "What went wrong here?" "What resources do you need?" "What are your own goals?" "What can I do to help?"

Keep in mind that the work bond is second only to family in its ability to tie people together. Create strong bonds through your caring leadership.

Remember: "Work" and "Life" are not two separate worlds. Keep them in balance together. Be the same consistent person; manifest the same values whether at home or at work.

General Instructions for Conducting a Values Gap Analysis

In preparing to do this exercise with a group, it is important to emphasize that this is a safe place, that nothing said will be held against the person making the statement. If the organization's top management cannot make this guarantee, then don't do the exercise. Without complete honesty—which requires a safe environment—the exercise will be worthless.

First, set up four flip charts in front of the room.

Write at the top of the first flip chart: *Institutional Values as We Would Like Them to Be.*

Ask the group to complete this sentence: "We want to work for an organization that values _____." Write the answers in a list. Don't worry about duplication or shadings of meaning, just write them down.

Write at the top of the second flip chart: *Personal Values as We Would Like Them to Be.*

Ask the group to complete this sentence: "We want to work with people who value _____." List the answers. There will be much duplication with the previous list. That's okay.

Write at the top of the third flip chart: *Institutional Values as They Are.*

Ask the group to complete this sentence: "*This* organization values _____. This will create a bit of tension in the room, and it will be more difficult for people to speak because it is in this exercise that negative values are often mentioned (such as, "The organization values overwork to the detriment of family life," etc.) You must encourage people to speak up, openly and honestly.

Write at the top of the fourth flip chart: *Personal Values as They Are.*

Ask the group to complete this sentence: "These people value_____." Explain that "these people" includes coworkers as well as management. Once again, this may be difficult for people to talk about openly.

After the exercise, you may want to adjourn for a while or even until the next day. Ask the group to consider the "gap" between the values as we want them and the values as they are.

At the next session, break into two groups, one for institutional values and one for personal values, and have them analyze the gap between the values and make a report for the larger group.

The objective of the exercise is not to close the gap immediately. That would be impossible. Rather it is to raise consciousness about where the organization and the people fall short in creating a workplace that reflects the values they themselves have said they most desire.

Two Useful Phrases for the Bulletin Board:

"Concentrate on the Human Value of the Dollar, and Not on the Dollar Value of the Human"

"Burnout Is Not a Crisis of Time....It Is a Crisis of the Spirit"

(Adapted from *Confessions of An Accidental Businessman*, Berrett-Koehler, Copyright 1996, James A. Autry).

Chapter Eight

LEARNING SERVANT-LEADERSHIP FROM NATIVE AMERICA—AGAIN

Lane Baldwin

One grandfather spends his life creating daycare centers while another is a history mentor. A couple works with a dozen volunteers to feed the elderly. Although these people are spread across the continent and were raised in different cultures, they share two common attributes: They're all Native American leaders, and they're all *servant-leaders*. Three decades ago, Robert Greenleaf changed the map of the business world after reading Herman Hesse's account of an indigenous servant-leader named Leo in *Journey to the East*. I've found many such leaders in the First Nations of Native America, and they have much to teach us about how we govern ourselves: who leads, who follows, and why. Perhaps more important are the lessons they can teach us about how to create a servant-led society. As our children grow, the leaders will rise to the call and the followers will know exactly whom to respect, a direct result of the group-led, generational education model used in traditional Native America.

I'm not suggesting we forsake modern society, selling everything we own to go live in the mountains. Rather, I propose the opposite: that we blend indigenous wisdom into the way we lead our society. We can also learn better methods to teach servant-leadership. If we study these lessons, we can embrace their secrets to create what Greenleaf hoped for: a more just society. Nevertheless, in order to look at the similarities between servant-leadership and traditional Native American leadership, we have to get beyond a few differences first.

A Clash of Cultures

Since Columbus first landed in North America, the dominant culture has found it difficult to understand the Native American Nations, and the reason is simple, if not obvious: the Nations were governed by servant-leaders. Far greater than the language barrier, servant-leadership was the broadest cultural chasm between two radically different cultures, rivaling the Grand Canyon in magnitude.

Imagine the confusion when the leader of an expedition, holder of title, rank, and power, steeped in European feudalism, asked to speak with the leader of a Native village. This lordly fellow and his entourage were led to a poorly dressed grandfather of a man, living in the smallest hut in the village. Often the explorer was led to a group of a dozen or more elders, and this only compounded the problem, increasing the explorer's disbelief and frustration. *What madness is this?* he might wonder. *I want to speak to the leader, not the village pauper.*

Obviously language was a significant barrier, but it was a hurdle the explorers eventually overcame, if only a little at a time. Once the explorer could communicate, he would seek to conduct his business. But harder than language to translate was a psychology of community considerably more foreign in nature. Pleading his case for use of land, or fishing and hunting rights, he hoped for a positive response. Instead, he was often asked to return in a few days or weeks because the leader had to seek consensus among the villagers before any action could be taken. All of the elders had to confer; consequences had to be assessed. The explorer might return in a few weeks or a month, only to be introduced to a different spokesperson for the group, instead of the previous leader. In a later interaction, still another elder might speak for the group, then another. The overall leadership was the same, but different leaders would accept responsibility for various issues or projects, each supported in their turn by the whole.

A direct result of European confusion with this fluid, service-

140

based government was the attempt to force a single "king" or "chief" on the community, which is why we read about Cherokee "princesses" even today, something that traditional Native Americans find amusing, or worse, derogatory to their culture. It saddens me to consider that our government did its best to destroy the excellent forms of servant-government in the First Nations. Native Americans have been forced to accept a more "modern," more "civilized" form of government. This may well be the most damaging action ever committed against them, made even worse by the savage irony that Jefferson and other founding fathers learned so much about representative democracy from the Iroquois Confederacy before destroying the communities that conceived it.

Searching for Common Ground

I was drawn to servant-leadership for the same reason I was drawn to return to my Native American heritage and traditions. At its core, servant-leadership is a very spiritual way of leading, and traditional Native American culture is a spiritual way of life. Robert Greenleaf often focused on the moral and ethical aspects of leadership. He, and the disciples who continue to follow him, frequently offers examples of true servant-leaders among spiritual or religious communities. Yet it is done in the same soft way as in traditional indigenous cultures. No heavy-handed salesmanship, very little quoting of scripture; simply a "walk the talk" attitude supported by stories that emphasize service to others. This "soft-sell" approach, a product of Greenleaf's Quaker roots, made it easy for me to digest and assimilate the essence of servant-leadership, refining and codifying concepts I'd been working with for years. It also made it easy to for me to find numerous role models in the history of the First Nations.

While reading my background material and preparing the original draft of this essay, I spent time reflecting silently as Greenleaf advised—another activity that mirrors the traditional mindset, another link between two worlds. My original intent had been simply to connect the dots between servant-leadership and traditional Native American ways, to show the similarities.

However, as I delved deeper, I discovered differences between the two cultures. I began to see that it's not just what, but *when and how*, we teach our children that matters. I've come to believe that indigenous societies can show us how to steep our children in the ethics of service, one generation after another. As I asked myself how we might better match our culture to theirs, I didn't come up with many "final answers," but I think I've found some ideas we can consider, and perhaps engage in dialogue over, in the servant-leadership community.

Keep in mind that this is a broad-stroke discussion of servant-leadership in traditional societies and may differ in details from what you might learn from any individual First Nation, or from the indigenous history of your distant ancestors. There are more than five hundred separate nations within "Native American" culture. Contrary to the new-age desire for a "pan-Indian" mono-culture, which is more easily marketed, it's impossible to lump them all together into a single set of cultural models. Each group of communities translated servant-leadership to its specific circumstances. With that said, let me tell you what I discovered when I superimposed the maps of two different cultures.

Two Maps of the Same Terrain

In his essay *On Character and Servant-Leadership: Ten Characteristics of Effective, Caring Leaders*, Larry Spears offers the traits crucial to success as a servant-leader that perfectly mirror the nature of a traditional indigenous leader. If you haven't already done so, it's well worth a visit to the Spears Center at www.spearscenter.org to read the full essay. I am grateful for Larry's permission to summarize his points and filter them through a Native American lens to illuminate my thoughts. For the sake of clarity, I have italicized his ten traits, and one sub-trait, in the following paragraph.

A leader who *listens* carefully to the community, and with *empathy*, can understand the will of the group. This leader actively seeks opportunities for *healing* in interpersonal and intercommunal relationships. *Awareness*, including *self-awareness*, is critical to understanding the most important issues facing the servant-leader, especially concerning ethics and values. *Persuasion* rather than coercion is paramount if the servant-leader is to build consensus in the community. *Conceptualization* requires the servant-leader to think beyond the short-term, considering the consequences of all actions upon the long-term future of the community. Servant-leaders cultivate *foresight* in order to apply the lessons of history to the realities of the present and to a compelling vision of the future in such a way as to recognize the probable outcome of the actions about to be taken. Native Americans know well that *stewardship* means actions are taken only in the best interests of those to come. Their leaders are committed to the *growth of people*, actively seeking to understand each person's special gifts, and providing the means to nurture them. Finally, the servant-leader knows that *building community* will result in a synergism that will benefit every individual.

As I look back on the great servant-leaders throughout Native American history, it's clear to me that each of them possessed most, if not all, of these traits. Robert Greenleaf taught that service was the foundation for true leadership. This famous quote is one of the cornerstones of his philosophy: "The servant-leader is servant first....It begins with the natural feeling that one wants to serve, to serve first."[1]

Greenleaf's chant of *servant first, servant always*, echoes the words a healer or holy man might sing. The history of Native America is filled with servant-leaders for one reason: no one could lead until they proved their willingness to serve. This included their village leaders (government), holy men (clergy), healers (doctors), hunt leaders, farmers and herders (businessmen), warriors (military), and more. Their young were raised in this environment of service; it was part of daily life. They constantly saw the adults serve, and as the children grew, they were encouraged to actively seek their own ways to serve the community. Their first forays into leadership might come when, having conceived a project too large or difficult to handle alone, they asked their peers to help them. If the youngster enjoyed some standing among his age group, based on his willingness to serve others, he would receive help. If he didn't, he was on his own. You can see how a child in that environment would learn quickly that service is of the utmost importance, and, as they grew, they would naturally serve in larger ways, some as leaders, and some as followers. From cradle to grave they would be *servants first—servants always*.

The servant-leaders who work tirelessly to preserve Native American culture today continue to demonstrate these same traits on a daily basis. One modern-day servant-leader has spent his entire life teaching Native communities how to set up day-care services for their children. When I met him, he was paying his bills by delivering pizzas thirty hours a week and spent another sixty hours each week on the centers. Barely making enough to survive, he refused to work more hours because it would take time from the day-care programs. In his spare time, he visits elders in his community, often bringing food, clothing, and other necessities. He chops wood for them and does other heavy chores so they won't have to. When asked why he spends so much time helping others, his answer is simple. "This is what life is about: service to others." And yes, he is regarded as a leader in his community, having gathered many followers from those he's mentored in day-care operations, from the children who have grown up in the centers and the communities they support. And they are servant-leaders as well as servant-followers.

Another anonymous friend has spent his life protecting the original teachings. Focusing on pre-contact beliefs, traditions, and ceremony, he has amassed a volume of material that would make any anthropologist green with envy. This mission takes most of his time, and most of his money as well. He spends countless hours each week patiently instructing the next generation, inculcating them in a culture of service. Again, he is growing servant-leaders and servant-followers.

Each week, a thirty-something couple travels a circuit hundreds of miles long to deliver food, clothing, and other supplies to elders in their widely dispersed community. They live simply, preferring to invest their time and money into caring for the elders that protect and perpetuate the ancient ways of their people. Over the years, they've gathered dozens of followers who help them in their work and learn from the elders. Studying this group's relationships reveals at least complex and fully realized levels of servant-leadership and servant-followership woven into the tapestry of community.

These are just a few of the servant-leaders among the Native American traditionalists living on the edge of our modern, technological society. They are proof positive that, even in the most difficult circumstances, it's still possible to pass the torch of servant-leadership to the generations to come. I believe servant-leadership is similar to the traditional Native American leadership model, the two following many of the same general contours, and that Native American success with passing servant culture from one generation to the next deserves investigation. If so, we can look beyond the actual subject matter being taught and consider what else we can learn.

Teaching Servant-Leadership

One major difference between the two cultures is *when* servant-leadership education begins. Currently our children begin to learn about it in college, if at all. Some children receive a brief introduction to the concept in high school wrapped in encouragement to investigate further. In contrast, Native American children begin to receive training at age one or two; it continues throughout their lives. The benefits of this seem obvious, so how can we emulate this? Let's start with what we have.

We've made significant headway at the university level in the past several decades. For example, I'm very pleased to report that the University of Richmond's Jepson School of Leadership Studies not only weaves servant-leadership throughout its entire undergraduate program in leadership studies, it also features a specific course on service to society. Celebrating its seventeenth anniversary this year, the Jepson School has been working to introduce servant-leadership to high school students. Students visit high schools during the school year to increase awareness of servant-leadership and its importance to our society. Their first-of-its-kind degree in leadership studies and their drive into high schools place the Jepson School at the vanguard of servant-leadership education.

There are many other schools addressing socially responsible business practices, and we should commend each of them for their efforts and cheer their successes. But shouldn't *every* institution of higher learning, *especially schools of management,* be teaching servant-leadership? Wouldn't it be wonderful if every management school in the country offered such a curriculum by the end of this decade? But that still wouldn't be enough, even though it would complete work that's been going on for more than two decades. It isn't enough because it's not *early* enough.

We can improve our results by actively seeking more ways to promote servant-leadership to high school students as the Jepson School is doing, and to teach our children at even younger ages the value of service to others, reaching all the way back into grade school and before. Numerous possibilities exist, from school activities such as student government, honors programs, sports, music, arts, and clubs, to outside activities such as spiritual programs, athletics clubs, martial arts training (another hidden treasure trove of servant-leaders), boys and girls clubs, and more.

We can emulate Native American successes by teaching our children, from the time they can walk, that service to others is the highest calling to which one can aspire. Teaching servant-leadership to children in their earliest school years isn't as farfetched as it may seem. Six Seconds, a nonprofit organization that promotes emotional intelligence education, has programs that reach children of all ages. Research supports the success of their programs, and the teaching methods are flowing across the nation one school at a time. What's more, because emotional intelligence is an integral part of servanthood, and the two are so obviously compatible, it seems that the methods required to teach them would be compatible, as well. At the forefront of learning a life of servant-leadership, I envision many teachers taking up the challenge to develop a curriculum that spans all schools, all ages.

Finding the Right Teachers

We can't leave this critical education to our schools alone, however. Nor should they be the sole foundation of our efforts. Teachers polish and add to the lessons our children learn, but they are not sole providers. But if it's true that teachers are just one part of the collective of educators, then *who* will teach our children servant-leadership? The adage "it takes a village to raise a child" has a distinct indigenous flavor, but let's go one step at a time to get there. First, children need to see service in the proper light, and that begins with the parents. How we act while we perform service for others, and how we interact with those who serve us teach our children lessons every day. Individually, and *as a society*, how many of those lessons do you think are the right ones?

When serving the family, we can practice without preaching, walking our talk in bold steps every day. Often, when I speak to groups about finding fulfillment through service, I talk about the joy we can feel by holding our daily chores in a slightly different light. Doing the laundry or washing the dishes, mowing the lawn or taking out the trash—all of these are acts of service to the family as a unit, the most basic unit of community. This is one small secret to my own personal happiness and I think it's helpful to anyone who wishes to try it. But my point here is that our children see, hear, *and understand*, far more than we give them credit for. So when they hear us grumble about making dinner, or see us scowl our way through any of the dozens of tasks required to maintain our home, *our community*, they're learning an entirely different lesson than we intend to teach. In order to do what indigenous communities do, we must offer impeccable models to our children as much as possible. *We* are the most important teachers of the lessons of service. We can then build on this early, basic training so that, as our children grow, they will be immersed in a life of service to others, coming to know and even thrive on the fulfillment that service brings.

Finding the Time to Teach

In general, the amount of "hands-on" time an indigenous parent gives to children is significantly greater than in modern society. This is a critical lynchpin of success for the program, and thankfully, many parents are already making changes that will help. In the workplace, we've seen a marked increase in parents of all ages and both sexes actively seeking ways to mold their careers around the responsibilities of holistic family life. We're seeing a dramatic shift in perspective back to the belief that family should be the focus of our lives and that means it deserves more energy, and *more time* than we've allowed ourselves in the recent past. (Remember, it wasn't so long ago that parents had twice as much time for their children than we do today.) The business world is beginning to respond to this trend, experimenting with telecommuting, in-office daycare, floating shifts, and other techniques.

Having spent much of my time in the world of retail, there's another growing trend that's dear to my heart: businesses that voluntarily close on Sundays, even though they lose significant amounts of business. In central Texas, McCoy's Hardware stores brag that they do a different kind of building on Sundays—that's when they build families. I remember standing near the front of my local McCoy's listening to a customer comment about that very policy, and to the manager's patient explanation that their employees needed time with their families, too, and that their children were in school during the week, and their spouses at work, just as the customer's were. Two years later, I listened to the same discussion in a Ukrops grocery store in Richmond, Virginia, with different actors in the roles. The owners of these two chains sacrifice profit to provide a great service to their employees, proving that servant-leadership can be practiced— and taught—on many levels, in many ways.

After briefly addressing parental time priorities, we may again ask *who else* will teach our children. In a traditional society, there are numerous elders to teach, to guide, *to demonstrate* servant-leadership beginning at the child's birth and continuing throughout his or her entire life. Supporting the parents, the second line of teachers are other adults within the extended family. These might include aunts, uncles, grandparents and great-grandparents, and cousins to several degrees. Supporting them are the adults of the other extended families in that village. The interesting thing is that, for the most part, the adults within a specific community all follow the same guidelines and the same methods to teach service as the basis of all relationships. Therefore, while a child might spend time with numerous adults or groups of adults learning different skills, the child was constantly learning about service from *every teacher*. This continuity seems to be a crucial aspect of generational education. Perhaps part of our answer lies in returning to child-rearing as a community effort. We're beginning to see parents gathering in unique ways to share responsibilities among several families, creating instant "uncles" and "aunts" for the children involved. Home schooling networks deserve consideration. Imagine sharing educational responsibilities with a dozen other families, all of whom teach *and live* servant-leadership. We might also reconsider the benefits of a multigenerational family living very close together. An extended family inhabiting a series of houses in a subdivision, or a collection of apartments in a building, would be a modern-day equivalent of ancient village life.

Where We Need Servant-Leaders Most

Imagine an entire generation raised from the cradle on servant-leadership. Furthermore, with each successive generation, their numbers will grow until, after several generations, we will have raised an entire society as servants to themselves. What might the changes be in our government, education, religion, and business? And while servant-leaders benefit all types of institutions, it is in the realm of politics that we will need them most, if this vision is to succeed to its fullest. Because our elected officials are among our most trusted servant-leaders, holding our essential liberties in their hands, these positions require servants with only the best intentions *for the whole* in their hearts and minds. And there is much to learn about this from Native Americans; the entire Native American system was designed to attract only those who were willing to sacrifice everything for their community. That's why the lordly explorer, his court and soldiers, was led to a group of impoverished elders to conduct community business. These elders had given away almost everything as part of their daily practice of sacrifice for others. Imagine that level of surrender to the whole somehow blended into our current political arena. What the founders of this country learned once, we must learn again. For the most part, what Jefferson studied so well quickly vanished like a wisp of smoke on the wind, and took its own time coming back. Pockets of it remained, such as in the

Society of Friends, who ultimately grew a modern-day prophet of humanistic business management and communal service. But if the servant-leaders elsewhere in our society are to succeed, they will need like-minded individuals in the city, state, and federal halls of politics. How else to put an end to the negative energy of destructive competition and in-fighting that paralyzes proper action? What better replacement than a positive, cooperative sense of doing what is right for everyone in the community, no matter how large or small? If you agree, then the question again becomes one of *how*. And the answer is simple: we do what Native American societies did for thousands of years; we grow a society of individuals that will only accept servant-leaders.

The Benefits of Servant-Followership

If we are to enjoy true servants in our governments, *servant-followers* must elect them. As Greenleaf pointed out, in order to create a servant-led society, true servant-followership must emerge. And perhaps their most important service is to choose the right leaders. Servant-leaders won't help society nearly as much if that society doesn't understand their importance. This next generation (and those beyond) must learn to avoid the mistake of "settling." Our society has learned to settle—we settle for the lesser of two evils, we settle for a coarser society, we settle a dozen times a day and don't even notice we're doing it. But our children can't afford that, if generational education in servant-leadership is to work. The followers must support the right people, thereby doing their part to serve the interests of society. In politics more than anything, we can't afford to settle for a person who isn't right for the job. It will be up to us to elect the right person.

As we are raising a generation of servant-leaders, we can teach that same generation about the true nature of *servant-followership*, teach them whom to follow and why. Certainly the potential for gain in other institutions is as great as it is for politics, and these other centers of leadership will benefit from an entire generation raised in the ethics of servant-leadership. However, it is in the realm of politics that the most altruistic leaders can do the most good, that the least altruistic can do the most damage. In this, I agree with the Nations.

A Cause for Reflection

We've looked—*very briefly*—at servant-leadership through the filter of Native America, repeating Jefferson's studies, and perhaps seen a new way of educating our young to become leaders and followers in service. Will any of this be easy? Absolutely not. But the rewards are great. Depending on how long it takes for the concepts to be discussed, expanded upon, refined, and put into process in communities around the nation, we could see the first gains by the end of this decade. I can think of no better way to open the new millennium, than to bring the ethics of servant-leadership to an entirely different audience, a younger one, in a new way. It will take a few generations, even several, to achieve the proper mass and momentum. Our society will need to learn a new definition of *long-term* in order to make these ideas work to the fullest. Rather than thinking about tomorrow, or perhaps our children's future, we need to think about the lives of our grandchildren's grandchildren and beyond. The rewards to society are more than worth the long-term planning, the effort repaid many times over in so many ways.

The leaders will come, I'm sure. Many will come if we teach them young and teach them well. The rest will be servant-followers and will be just as important because only they can choose the best servant-leaders. We can learn again from our Native American brothers and sisters, their model of servant-leadership, their teaching methods, and their way of bringing it to their government.

In closing, I invite you to join me in my next activity. Having finished writing this, I'm going to reflect on these thoughts as I watch the sun set. I think—*I hope*—that both Greenleaf and the grandfathers will be pleased.

Chapter Nine

CLARIFYING INTENTION AS THE PATH TO SERVANT-LEADERSHIP

Maren Showkeir and Jamie Showkeir

The scene is familiar, reproduced in books, stories, movies, and television sitcoms. From his armchair in the living room, the stern father confronts the nervous, fidgeting date with this question: "What, exactly, are your intentions toward my daughter?"

At its heart, the question is designed to get the young man to reflect on how he will *behave* toward the young woman (although in today's modern society, populated with independent women who often initiate relationships, it's an equally legitimate question for both genders). Are they two friends out for a fun evening with a genial companion? Are they hoping to develop a deeper relationship? Are their intentions to satisfy carnal desires with a temporary tryst? Is the intention to scout a potential life partner?

Note that the archetypal father, however, doesn't frame the question in terms of behavior. He specifically asks about intention, because that is what will drive every single decision the young people make while they're on the date. It is intention that infuses meaning in all behavior. Consider that Dr. Christiaan Barnard, who pioneered open-heart surgery, and Jack the Ripper, who murdered prostitutes, engaged in almost identical behavior—they cut people open with a scalpel. It was their radically different intentions that set their behavior apart.

Unless we get clear about our intentions, we go through life unaware of its connection to our actions, behaviors, and the way we engage others. By concentrating solely on behavior as a means for achieving our ends, we are unconscious about the very thing that drives us. It's like setting out on a journey with only the vaguest idea of the destination and no idea of what lies between where we are and where we want to go. Without a clear vision (intention) of where we intend to arrive, almost any old route will do.

By pondering some version of "Who do I want to be in this world?" we can develop a guiding awareness of whether we are choosing behaviors that conform to our intentions in any given circumstance. Who I am (being) proceeds and influences what I do (action.) As author and lecturer Wayne Dyer points out: "*Intention sets our reality.*"[1]

Most great leaders understand the power of clear intention, whether their intentions lead to destruction and repression or foster progress and freedom. Look at the contrast of intentions from two charismatic leaders in the mid-twentieth century.

Adolph Hitler was clear in his intention of creating a master race by "cleansing" the genetic pool through extermination of those deemed to be inferior, including Jews, homosexuals, gypsies, and people with disabilities. All his decisions for action—conquering neighboring countries, building concentration camps, mass murder—were filtered through his intention of creating a "pure race." He continued on his course despite the toll to his country and general world opinion that rejected everything he stood for.

Mohandas Gandhi was equally focused on his intention to achieve self-determination for the people of India and eliminate British imperialism through nonviolent means. His clarity of purpose and the intentionality of his spirit served as a constant lens for determining how he engaged others, and allowed him to remain steadfast to his vision even as he suffered the most grueling hardships. His laser-like focus energized the tactics, methods, and techniques he chose for achieving his objectives. Honoring intention helped him remain strong and determined, even when he was treated as a third-class citizen and beaten by the police, and even when he endured several prison terms. He nearly starved himself to death in the name of nonviolent reform. His vision of nonviolence inspired others: Gandhi's followers staggered under the blows of the British military, but they honored his intention by refusing to strike back. Other great leaders, including Martin Luther King, turned to Gandhi's example in creating their own intentions for change through nonviolent means.

Gandhi is a venerated man whose life has inspired millions and Hitler is a despised figure in world history for his murderous, despotic tactics, but undeniably, their proficiency in aligning actions with intention gave them a common trait.

Be the change you want to see in the world is a statement attributed to Gandhi, and is a statement of intention. Those words place the focus squarely where it belongs: Real change springs from the individual, and influence is best wielded with clear intentions.

In their book *Spiritual Capital*, Danah Zohar and Ian Marshall illuminate the importance of intention:

> The awareness that I...have a deep center and that I need to be in contact with it and to act through it, confers meaning and authenticity to my projects and actions. It is exhilarating to know that I have an internal compass and that I can be led by its sense of direction. This is one crucial meaning of integrity—to act in accord with my internal compass.[2]

Establishing that "internal compass"—what we call intention—has deep implications for those seeking to be leaders, and is an essential exercise for those who are looking to become servant-leaders or who want to improve their effectiveness as a servant-leader.

Intention and Technique

In our work as consultants, we often get questions such as these: "How do I become a servant-leader? How can I acquire the skills? How do I learn the process? Can you give me a list of steps or techniques?"

Processes, methods, and techniques are important aspects of leadership, but taken in isolation, they lack the necessary framework to create true transformation. Developing techniques without a clear intention is like demanding the fuel before we have built the engine. A personal transformation process is ignited by deeply reflecting on our purpose.

Intentions can spring from sources ranging from the divine to the practical. They can be grounded in deeply held spiritual beliefs or originate from abiding moral principles or from resonant philosophies. They can be born from a desire to improve oneself, one's community, or the world. Intentions can be as overarching as Gandhi's, as broad as leading an organization in ways that are both ethical and profitable, or as specific as completing a project with the use of true collaboration. For the purposes of this chapter, we are focusing on intentions that inspire positive change (Gandhi, Dr. Christiaan Barnard) as opposed to those that are self-serving or destructive (Hitler, Jack the Ripper).

Specifically, we are addressing the *intention* to be of service as the first and most prominent element of servant-leadership.

The Intentions of the Servant-Leader

Robert K. Greenleaf, after spending forty years researching management development and education at AT&T, became convinced that the authoritarian, command-and-control leadership so prominent in U.S. corporations was not only ineffective, but also ran counter to ethical human behavior. After taking early retirement in 1964, he created the Center for Applied Ethics with the intention of shifting the paradigm of power-centered leadership to a model that used service as a way to distribute personal power to everyone. He coined the term *servant-leader* and until his death in 1990, he worked tirelessly to extol the virtues of service and create servant-leaders. Greenleaf manifested his intention for servant-leadership with this statement: *The servant- leader is servant-first. It begins with the natural feeling that one wants to serve, to serve first.*[3]

In Greenleaf's biography, the introduction states: *The core idea of servant-leadership is quite simple: authentic, ethical leaders, those whom we want to follow, are servants first. This is a matter of intent, action, skills, capacities and being.*[4]

This statement outlines the logical process for becoming a true leader. First, be clear about your intent, and then align your actions, skills, capacities, and ways of being with that intention.

The primacy of Greenleaf's intention was recognized and clarified well before he began employing techniques to live out his vision. This clarity helped him be thoughtful about the best ways to behave in accordance with his intention. In his book *Servant Leadership: A Journey into the Nature of Legitimate Power and Greatness*, he wrote:

> As long as one is leading, one always has a goal....The word "goal" is used in the special sense of the overarching purpose, the big dream, the visionary concept, the ultimate consummation which one approaches but never really achieves. It is something presently out of reach; it is something to strive for, to move toward or become.[5]

The crucial process of developing and honing intention is often overlooked by contemporary leaders, who view leadership as little more than a collection of techniques. The use of techniques, processes, methods, and skills is at the core of a vast array of modern literature written for people who want to establish themselves as leaders or become more effective leaders. In many cases, the underlying message is that in order to be powerful and effective, we must be armed with the latest methods. We must read the latest "How To" manuals and follow the trendiest "Eight Steps to Becoming a Great Leader."

To be sure, acquiring good techniques can help us become more competent leaders. We can employ techniques to develop skills such as organizing, listening, using our time efficiently, communicating, networking, strategizing, showing empathy, directing and wielding influence, and more. But without a clear intention, without defining who we want to be or what we want to create, these skills can become little more than tools for an unstated intention to manipulate others into complying with our wishes. Clearly, if our leadership intention is merely to gain compliance, many of the techniques advocated by leadership gurus today will provide a gentler, more benevolent way to command those we seek to lead. However, these techniques also defy the natural fact that people always have a choice about how to react to their circumstances, and controlling is not the same as leading. In Greenleaf's words, *The value of coercive power is inverse to its use.*[6] Greenleaf believed, and we are in emphatic agreement, that these sorts of manipulative techniques, combined with self-serving intentions, have helped create the leadership crises we are experiencing in the world today.

One prominent, oft-cited example of this kind of leadership failure can be seen in the rise and fall of Enron. Author and educator Marshall Goldsmith, who studied the use of values or vision statements in several major U.S. companies, said that the effort and financial resources that went into developing Enron's corporate statement of values produced materials that were "particularly noteworthy." In *strategy+business*, an online magazine published by the Harvard Business School, Goldsmith stated:

> I was greatly impressed by the company's espoused high-minded beliefs....It was one of the most smoothly professional presentations on ethics and values that I have ever seen. Clearly, Enron spent a fortune "packaging" these wonderful messages.[7]

However, Enron's highly publicized implosion revealed clear evidence that the behavior of Enron's top executives was clearly inconsistent with the intentions the corporate credo espoused. Put another way, the leaders never intended to create the kind of organization where values such as integrity, respect, and real shareholder value would be reflected in the actions of those who worked there.

Goldsmith and his partner Howard Morgan looked at more than 11,000 managers in eight major corporations to examine the effect of leadership development programs in changing executive behavior. Each company had different values (intentions) and different words to describe ideal leadership behavior, but none of them made any difference in the way leaders behaved, according to their study, published in 2004. Almost no correlation could be found between the words on the wall and the behavior of leaders, according to Goldsmith. When leaders' intentions are in conflict with the company-stated values, the leadership techniques and behaviors they choose make values statements look self-serving and manipulative at best, deceptive at worst.

Another example of intentions that conflict with techniques in the corporate world can be seen in the disparity between earnings of American CEOs compared to the wages of the labor force, which is the widest in the world. In 2006, CEOs of major U.S. companies collected as much money from one day on the job as average workers made over the entire year. These CEOs averaged $10.8 million in total compensation, the equivalent of over 364 times the pay of an average American worker. In the decade that ended in 2006, "CEO pay rose roughly 45 percent, adjusted for inflation. The real value of the minimum wage now stands 7 percent below the minimum wage's value in 1996."[8]

Significantly, these corporate executives' salaries are not connected to improved performance or better returns to shareholders. Leaders get paid even when their businesses are failing.

This clearly speaks to intention. If a leader's intention is to maximize personal wealth or to use monetary gain as a measure of worth, then they choose techniques to achieve that kind of compensation. While it's true that board members and consultants collude with this practice, it is ultimately the leader's decision to accept the salary even when it could run counter to the organization's best interest. (Self-interested intentions can also be seen during times of cost-cutting and layoffs—it is the rare CEO who returns or slashes his or her own salary.) How might behavior change if the CEO's intention was to run a collaborative company, where decisions about salaries and cost-cutting were made in cooperation with its employees?

If a corporate leader's primary intention is to focus on gaining market share or increasing stock prices at all cost, any technique used to undermine the competition could be considered fair game. This was reflected in the actions of leaders at British Airways, who set out to take customers away from Virgin Atlantic Airways in the early 1990s. British Airways used tactics such as invading Virgin Airways confidential files and calling customers who had purchased tickets on Virgin to offer them lower airfares if they would switch their reservations to British Airways. (Eventually the "dirty tricks" technique was exposed, and in 1993 British Airways agreed to pay Virgin Atlantic more than £600,000 in damages.) British Airways' techniques were derived from intention, even if the intentions were hidden.

On the other hand, if a leader's intention (stated or unstated) is to create an organization where everyone is treated justly, has ample individual opportunity to contribute regardless of rank and is paid fairly, techniques that foster personal greed, unethical tactics, and unfair practices will be repudiated.

Discovering Intentions

So where does intention come from? Put in today's leadership vernacular, "How do we get one?"

Webster defines *intention* as "a determination to act in a certain way," which connects vision to behavior or actions. Webster defines *determination* as "the act of deciding definitely and firmly." Taken together, the definitions provide a deeper understanding of what intention requires—definitely and firmly deciding to act in a certain way.

Being clear about who we want to be requires deep humility, honest introspection, and constant attention to creating self-awareness. It requires that we eschew self-deception and confront uncomfortable truths about ourselves. We have to shed our unconscious assumptions about who we are or what we want to accomplish. Meditation, objective self-assessment, and a willingness to be open to the feedback of others are invaluable tools on the path to self-awareness and clarifying intentions. As Zohar and Marshall point out: *Self-awareness is the paramount competency of emotional intelligence, but it is also the most difficult to achieve.*[9] In his book *Servant Leadership*, Greenleaf says essentially the same thing. *"What am I trying to do?"* is one of the easiest questions to ask and the most difficult to answer.[10]

One way to get clearer about our intentions is to invest time pondering questions such as these:

159

Who do I want to be in this world?

What is my purpose?

What am I trying to create?

What contributions do I want to make?

Why is it important for me, and others, to make these contributions?

What legacy would I like to leave?

Once we have wrestled with these powerful questions and developed satisfying answers, the questions of "how" we live out our intentions become more relevant, vital, and authentic. Techniques, methods, and processes are imbued with substance and meaning and provide ways to live out our vocation. Our determination to act in a certain way becomes firmer. That is where the work truly begins.

In the tradition of yoga, it is said that true spiritual growth comes not from new experiences, but from deconstructing the old habits that do not serve us. On this journey, when we embrace humility we listen deeply enough to find legitimate answers. To quote the late English actor George Arliss: *Humility is the only true wisdom by which we prepare our minds for all the possible changes of life.*[11]

Being humble enough to admit flaws publicly, regardless of our position, and being open to the necessary internal and external feedback for raising self-awareness is difficult. It calls for great character. And it is essential for the transformative process of aligning action with intention.

One way to make our intentions real and visible is to go public, not with an artificial "Statement of Values" but by sincerely explaining to others who we want to be and what we want to create. An explicit expression of our visions helps us hold ourselves accountable. It tells the world: "This is who I want to be; this is what I want to stand for." We can also invite others to give us feedback when our actions and intentions are incongruent. This sets the stage for powerful personal transformation.

Aligning Behavior with Intention

Thoughtful attention to our behavior and the way we engage others must constantly be filtered through the lens of our intention. This change can be particularly challenging in times of crisis, when we instinctively feel the pull and power of returning to old habits.

Chris Argyris, a professor emeritus at Harvard Business School, writes about this notion of aligning intention and action as "Espoused Theory vs. Theory in Use."[12] In decades of studying human behavior in organizations, he found that espoused theories were frequently in conflict with theories in use, and that people in organizations colluded with this conflict by remaining silent when they see this conflict occur.

For example, many companies in some form espouse the theory that "People are our most valuable resource." However, when it uses layoffs for cost-cutting, the company is making a clear statement that people are cost centers, not valuable resources. Most people understand that one is loath to eliminate something that is truly a "most valuable resource." By eliminating people's jobs, the organization's espoused theory, "People are our most valuable resource," conflicts with its theory in use. Layoffs tell folks that "Profits and higher stock prices are our most important priority, and people are overhead." We are not knocking the idea of companies being profitable—that is essential to survival. But in this example, layoffs would clearly be in conflict with the espoused theory.

We also see this incongruity in our consulting practice when we have been asked to help an organization with a change effort. When we go into an organization, leaders tell us that honesty and trust are core values. But when we ask to conduct interviews with workers to assess the issues in the organization, people insist on confidentiality because they don't trust that they can tell the truth without retribution. The espoused theory (we value honesty and trust) is in conflict with the theory in use (people get hammered for telling the truth). Employees see it as too risky and a career-threatening act to publicly state one's honest opinion.

This has serious implications in the discussion of how leaders align their intention and behavior. Those with clear intentions to create an organization that values honesty and trust must find techniques—ways of behaving—that will support that intention. Creating congruence also requires developing awareness, so that people are able to recognize when theories in use are incompatible with espoused theories and take responsibility for pointing it out. Awareness is the first step to altering behavior so that intention and technique are once again aligned. This is done not with the hope that others will embrace our example and take up our cause, because that, too, is manipulation. We choose behavior based only on who we want to be in the world. This creates leadership in which others can truly believe.

Defining and Clarifying our Intentions as Servant-leaders

After studying Greenleaf's writings, Larry Spears, president of the Spears Center for Servant-Leadership, gleaned Ten Characteristics of a Servant-Leader (see table). They are: listening, empathy, healing, awareness, persuasion, conceptualization, foresight, stewardship, commitment to the growth of others, and building community.

If we apply the questions of "Who do I want to be?" and/or "What do I want to create?" to each of these characteristics, we can see they all begin with intention.

Ten Characteristics of a Servant-Leader

Characteristic	Formulating Intention
Listening	I want to create in others an experience of being heard and understood.
Empathy	I want to demonstrate to others that I am sensitive to their unique experience.
Healing	I want to create ways to ease the pain of those who are hurting and make whole that which has come apart.
Awareness	I want to be attentive to my surroundings, my actions, and the effect of my behavior on others. I want to solicit and be open to feedback.

Persuasion	I want to build consensus by authentically representing my point-of-view while honoring and supporting others' views.
Conceptualization	I want to create and share visions for the whole and allow them to blossom through the input and efforts of others.
Foresight	I want to develop my intuition, follow my instincts, and prepare for the future by integrating thinking from the past and present.
Stewardship	I want to manage assets wisely and responsibly, always taking into account the good of the whole.
Commitment to Growth of Others	I want to actively create an environment where people are encouraged and supported as they develop their unique talents and maximize their potential.
Build Community	I want to create opportunities for inclusion and collaboration, embrace diversity, and acknowledge the innate freedom of others to choose accountability.

The examples in the table above are only one way of creating a set of formulating intentions that support becoming a servant-leader. Each partly answers the question, "Who do I want to be in this world?" Taken collectively, the intentions form an articulate statement that answers the question "What am I trying to create?" They provide a powerful framework through which I can direct my behavior and actions.

Formulating intentions that answer these two questions provides a litmus test for action and behavior and bolsters personal commitment to "being the change I want to see in the world." Practically speaking, if my intention is to create in others the experience of being heard and understood, I can no longer afford to wait impatiently for someone to stop speaking so I can argue my point and "win" the debate. More importantly, I have to be aware when this happens so I can alter my behavior so it is realigned with my intention. This becomes easier if I have taken the first step of making my intentions public and inviting others' feedback. By humbly considering feedback, solicited or unsolicited, I can integrate that learning into new future action.

Greenleaf offers another useful test to help servant-leaders determine whether intention and behavior are aligned. He refers to it as the Best Test: *Do those served grow as persons? Do they, while being served, become healthier, wiser, freer, more autonomous, more likely themselves to become servants? And what is the effect on the least privileged in society? Will they benefit or at least not be further deprived?*[13]

By creating actions based on the intentions behind the Ten Characteristics, servant-leaders breathe life into the notion that true leadership springs from "serving first." They engage others in ways that help them clarify their intentions, which leads to more individuals who are working in collaboration to improve the good of the whole.

A demonstration of how intentions, actions, and results create significant unity of leadership and character can be seen in the changes that emanated from the work done throughout the adult life of Brazilian leader Paulo Friere (1921–1997).[14]

Friere was raised by parents who prized dialogue (listening, empathy, conceptualization, persuasion) and respect for the autonomy and choices of others (awareness, building community, commitment to the growth of others). In the early 1960s, he became the first director of the University of Recife's Cultural Extension Service, but resisted the notion of defining "literacy" only as reading and writing skills. His intention was to create meaningful participation in society and the political process by embracing Brazil's peasant class. He focused his efforts on helping the peasants develop literacy about the political system in ways that gave them hope and the realization that they could have a significant voice in the day-to-day decisions that affected their lives (awareness, persuasion, stewardship, building community.) As this hope emerged, so did their realization of the necessity for reading, writing, and understanding the political system more fully. As this literacy grew, passivity and fatalism waned, and they began to see that their oppression wasn't inevitable. Through conscious action of engaging a political system that had long been closed to them, they became the source of their own dignity and freedom.

Friere never lost sight of his intentions, even when the Brazilian landowners maligned his work. When he was jailed for seventy days after a military coup, he stayed true to his intention by beginning his first major educational work, "Education as the Practice of Freedom." During a five-year exile in Chile, UNESCO acknowledged the adult education programs he helped create as being responsible for Chile's success in overcoming illiteracy—one of only five countries to receive this recognition.

He stayed true to his intention of creating a fairer and more just society. His actions focused on education as the means to permanent liberation. In the end, Friere's clarity of intention and the techniques he chose to make his vision real are what propelled him to pass Greenleaf's "Best Test."

True servant-leadership starts with an intention, in this case an intention to "serve first." Though the world seems incessantly focused on service—customer service, quality service, high levels of service—being a "servant" is not an aspiration that gets much voice. The time has come for understanding that we can't create for others what we can't do for ourselves. We can't provide customer service (or any other marketplace service) if we don't know what it is to be a servant. It will no longer suffice to view leadership as a collection of techniques. Reframing this notion is in itself an act of leadership—servant-leadership. Zohar and Marshall call it connecting with our "internal compass." Greenleaf called it a "natural feeling." We call it clarifying your intentions.

There is nothing new under the sun. B. C. Patanjali, the Indian philosopher credited with codifying the ancient practice of yoga, said:

> When you are inspired by some great purpose, some extraordinary project, all your thoughts break their bonds: your mind transcends limitations, your consciousness expands in every direction, and you find yourself in a new, great, and wonderful world. Dormant forces, faculties and talents become alive, and you discover yourself to be a greater person by far than you ever dreamed yourself to be.

The challenge for each of us is to find that great purpose by looking inward.

Chapter Ten

THE POWER OF A HYPHEN: THE PRIMACY OF SERVANTHOOD IN SERVANT-LEADERSHIP

David Wallace

This essay addresses the significance of including the hyphen in the terms servant-leader and servant-leadership. The primacy of servanthood in servant-leadership is supported by the use of the hyphen when that and its related term, servant-leader, are written. We would do well to consider using the hyphen when writing these terms, as a way of affirming the primacy of servanthood in servant-leadership.

Use of the Hyphen in the Literature

A cursory examination of servant-leadership literature reveals that in most cases, no hyphen is used in the written term: we write about *servant leaders* and *servant leadership*. However, a few writers (Larry Spears, for example) insert the hyphen, thus, *servant-leader* and *servant-leadership*.

Is there significance in the use of the hyphen? In private correspondence, Larry Spears has confirmed to me that his use of the hyphen is intentional, largely for the reasons described in this paper. I will not presume to speak for anyone other than myself regarding the intentionality of its presence or absence. Perhaps we haven't yet given it thought. But I propose that the hyphen has significance, though we may not have yet considered the possibility.

Grammatical Significance of the Hyphen

There *is* a difference between *servant leadership* and *servant-leadership*. To make the difference clearer, let us first consider what is perhaps the more fundamental term: *servant-leader*. Thus, the difference can be framed as a contrast between the *servant leader* and the *servant-leader*.

Grammatically, the one phrase (servant leader) is formed by a noun (servant) functioning as an adjective that modifies another noun (leader). The other phrase is a compound noun formed by the joining of two coequal nouns—coequal in at least a grammatical sense.

What is the difference? What weight does a hyphen have? The hyphen, in this case, serves to contrast two approaches to servant-leadership. In one type (the servant leader), the starting point is leadership: servant leadership is one kind of leadership. This approach is consistent with the grammatical form of the term: an adjective (functionally) *servant* modifying a noun *leadership*. In such grammatical constructions, primacy naturally falls to the noun.

In the other case (the servant-leader), there is a paradox formed by the joining of two sharply contrasting roles: servant and leader. The hyphen serves to eliminate the primacy of the second noun by removing the adjectival function of the first noun. Thus, the grammar of the unhyphenated construction supports the primacy of leadership, while in the hyphenated form, no such primacy emerges.

While the grammar of the hyphenated form does not give primacy to either noun, such a construction is more consistent with primacy resting with servant than the unhyphenated phrase. Describing one as *servant-leader* gives room for the proper primacy to be placed on *servanthood*, rather than leadership.

The Primacy of Servanthood

In servant-leadership studies, we return often to the formative statement of Robert Greenleaf: "The servant-leader is servant first. It begins with the natural feeling that one wants to serve. Then conscious choice brings one to aspire to lead."[1] If we take this statement seriously, we must acknowledge that servanthood, or service, comes first, and leadership follows.

This priority on servanthood in servant-leadership has profound significance. It sets servant-leadership apart from other forms of leadership. Other types of leadership are defined in the context of leadership. In contrast, servant-leadership is first an expression of servanthood, not simply a way of leading. Servant-leaders are servants first, then leaders.

If the primacy of servanthood in servant-leadership is not maintained, servant-leadership might be approached as simply a technique, a way of approaching leadership that in some cases might best fulfill organizational goals. This denies the very nature and heart of the servant-leader.

Of course, we cannot lean on grammar alone to support the primacy of servanthood in servant-leadership. We must affirm that primacy in other ways. Nonetheless, considering the use of the hyphen in the constructions *servant-leader* and *servant-leadership* provides an opportunity to affirm the primacy of servanthood in the very way we write the terms.

Conclusion

In a lineup of stellar essays representing careful and painstaking research and dealing with weighty issues related to servant-leadership, why wrangle over the significance of a hyphen? I suggest two reasons. First, considering the hyphen provides an opportunity for us to affirm the primacy of servanthood in servant-leadership. Secondly, it serves as a call to consider using the hyphen in our literature more consistently, as both a reminder of our own affirmation of the primacy of servanthood and a means of communicating that primacy, however subtly, in our writing.

Seeking to insert the hyphen may bring us into conflict with editors, at least in the case of *servant-leadership*. Experts in English grammar seem to agree that the rules prohibit the use of the hyphen in the construction servant-leadership, while allowing it in *servant-leader*.

Whether the battle with editors is worth fighting seems best left to individual judgment in the specific situations in which they arise. But I would suggest that when it is possible, we affirm the primacy of servanthood in servant-leadership by using the hyphen in both terms, *servant-leader* and *servant-leadership*.

Chapter Eleven
HOW IS YOUR LEADERSHIP CHANGING?
Margaret Wheatley

I'm sad to report that in the past few years, ever since uncertainty became our insistent twenty-first century companion, leadership has taken *a great leap backward* to the familiar territory of command and control. Some of this was to be expected, because humans usually default to the known when confronted with the unknown. Some of it was a surprise, because so many organizations had focused on innovation, quality, learning organizations, and human motivation. How did they fail to learn that whenever you impose control on people and situations, you only succeed in turning people into noncreative, shut-down, and cynical workers?

The Destructive Impact of Command and Control

The dominance of command and control is having devastating impacts. There has been a dramatic increase in worker disengagement, few organizations are succeeding at solving problems, and leaders are being scapegoated and fired.

Most people associate command and control leadership with the military. Years ago, I worked for the U.S. Army Chief of Staff. I, like most people, thought I'd see command and control leadership there. *The great irony is that the military learned long ago that, if you want to win, you have to engage the intelligence of everyone involved in the battle.* The Army had a visual reminder of this when, years ago, they developed new tanks and armored vehicles that traveled at unprecedented speeds of fifty miles an hour. When first used in battle during the first Gulf War, several times troops took off on their own, speeding across the desert at high speed. However, according to Army doctrine, tanks and armored vehicles must be accompanied by a third vehicle that literally is called the Command and Control vehicle. This vehicle could only travel at twenty miles an hour. (They have since corrected this problem.)

For me, this is a familiar image—people in the organization ready and willing to do good work, wanting to contribute their ideas, ready to take responsibility, and leaders holding them back, insisting that they wait for decisions or instructions. The result is dispirited employees and leaders wondering why no one takes responsibility or gets engaged anymore. In these troubled, uncertain times, we don't need more command and control; we need better means to engage everyone's intelligence in solving challenges and crises as they arise.

We Know How to Create Smart, Resilient Organizations

We do know how to create workplaces that are flexible, smart, and resilient. We have known for more than half a century that engaging people, and relying on self-managed teams, is far more productive than any other form of organizing. In fact, productivity gains in self-managed work environments are *at minimum thirty-five percent higher* than in traditionally managed organizations. And workers know this to be true when they insist that they can make smarter decisions than those delivered from on high.

With so much evidence supporting the benefits of participation, why isn't every organization using self-managed teams to cope with turbulence? Instead, organizations increasingly are cluttered with control mechanisms that paralyze employees and leaders alike. Where have all these policies, procedures, protocols, laws, and regulations come from? And why do we keep creating more, even as we suffer from the terrible consequences of overcontrol?

Even though worker capacity and motivation are destroyed when leaders choose power over productivity, it appears that bosses would rather be in control than have the organization work well. And this drive for power is supported by the belief that the higher the risk, the more necessary it is to hold power tightly. What's so dangerous about this belief is that just the opposite is true. Successful organizations, including the military, have learned that the higher the risk, the more necessary it is to engage everyone's commitment and intelligence. When leaders hold onto power and refuse to distribute decision making, they create slow, unwieldy, Byzantine systems that only increase risk and irresponsibility. We never effectively control people or situations by these means; we only succeed in preventing intelligent, fast responses.

The personal impact on leaders' morale and health is also devastating. When leaders take back power, when they act as heroes and saviors, they end up exhausted, overwhelmed, and deeply stressed. It is simply not possible to solve singlehandedly the organization's problems; there are just too many of them! One leader who led a high-risk chemical plant spent three years creating a highly motivated, self-organizing workforce. He described it this way: "Instead of just me worrying about the plant, I now have nine hundred people worrying. And coming up with solutions I never could have imagined."

Sometimes leaders fail to involve staff out of some warped notion of kindness. They don't include people; they don't share their worries, because they don't want to add to their stress. But such well-meaning leaders only create more problems. When leaders fail to engage people in finding solutions to problems that affect them, staffs don't thank the leader for not sharing the burden. Instead, they withdraw, criticize, worry, and gossip. They interpret the leader's exercise of power as a sign that he or she doesn't trust them or their capacities.

Assessing Changes in Your Leadership

With no time to reflect on how they might be changing, with no time to contemplate whether their present leadership is creating an effective and resilient organization, too many leaders drift into command and control, wondering why nothing seems to be working, angry that no one seems motivated anymore.

If you are feeling stressed and pressured, please know that this is how most leaders feel these days. Yet it is important that you take time to notice how your own leadership style has changed in response to the pressures of this uncertain time. Otherwise, you may end up disappointed and frustrated, leaving a legacy of failure rather than of real results.

Some Questions to Think About

Here are questions to help you notice if your leadership is slipping into command and control. If you feel courageous, circulate these questions and talk about them with staff.

1. What has changed in the way you make decisions? Have you come to rely on the same group of advisors? Do you try to engage those who have a stake in the decision?
2. What's happening to staff motivation? How does it compare to a few years ago?
3. How often do you find yourself invoking rules, policies, or regulations to get staff to do something?
4. How often do you respond to a problem by developing a new policy?
5. What information are you no longer sharing with staff? Where are you more transparent?
6. What's the level of trust in your organization right now? How does this compare to two to three years ago?
7. When people make mistakes, what happens? Are staff encouraged to learn from their experience? Or is there a search for someone to blame?

8. What's the level of risk-taking in the organization? How does this compare to two to three years ago?
9. How often have you reorganized in the past few years? What have you learned from that?
10. How are your personal energy and motivation these days? How does this compare to a few years ago?

SOURCES

"Servant-Leadership: Healing the Person, Healing the World," is an original essay created for this collection by Shann Ray Ferch. A portion of the essay first appeared in *The International Journal of Servant-Leadership*. Copyright © 2009 Shann Ray Ferch. Printed with permission of the author.

"Creating an Alternative Future," was a keynote presentation at the Greenleaf Center for Servant-Leadership international conference and was revised for this collection by Peter Block. Copyright © 2009 Peter Block. Printed with permission of the author.

"Introduction: The Spirit of Servant-Leadership," is an original essay created for this collection by Larry C. Spears. Copyright © 2009 Larry C. Spears. Printed with permission of the author.

"Servant-Leadership and the Interior of the Leader," is an original essay created for this collection by Shann Ray Ferch. Copyright © 2009 Shann Ray Ferch. Printed with permission of the author.

"César E. Chávez: Servant-Leadership in Action," is an original essay created for this collection by María D. Ortíz. Copyright © 2009 María D. Ortíz. Printed with permission of the author.

"The Welcoming Servant-Leader," is an original essay created for this collection by Jan Gunnarsson and Olle Blohm. Copyright © 2009 Jan Gunnarsson and Olle Blohm. Printed with permission of the authors. The essay is adapted from chapter 4 of *The Welcoming Leader*. Copyright © 2007, Jan Gunnarsson and Olle Blohm. Published in Swedish as *Den tjänande ledaren. Konsten att skapa välkomnande företag och platser* by Dialogos Förlag, Stockholm, Sweden.

"The Management Development Legacy of Robert K. Greenleaf,"

is an original essay created for this collection by Jeff McCollum and Joel Moses. Copyright © 2009 Jeff McCollum and Joel Moses. Printed with permission of the authors.

"Coaching for Servant-Leadership: Expanding the Capacity to Reflect from the Heart," is an original essay created for this collection by Deborah V. Welch with Virginia Duncan Gilmore. Copyright © 2009 Deborah V. Welch with Virginia Duncan Gilmore. Printed with permission of the authors.

"Holistic Servant-Leadership," is an original essay created for this collection by George SanFacon and Larry C. Spears. Copyright © 2009 George SanFacon and Larry C. Spears. Printed with permission of the authors.

"Bearing Witness: Insights for Servant-Leaders," is an original essay created for this collection by James A. Autry. Copyright © 2009 James A. Autry. Printed with permission of the author.

"Learning Servant-Leadership from Native America—Again," is an original essay created for this collection by Lane Baldwin. Copyright © 2009 Lane Baldwin. Printed with permission of the author.

"Clarifying Intention as a Servant-Leader," is an original essay created for this collection by Maren Showkeir and Jamie Showkeir. Copyright © 2009 Maren Showkeir and Jamie Showkeir. Printed with permission of the authors.

"The Power of a Hyphen," is an original essay created for this collection by David Wallace. Copyright © 2008 David Wallace. Printed with permission of the author.

"How Is Your Leadership Changing?" as well as the two poems included in the essay, are original works by Margaret Wheatley and first appeared in the *International Journal of Servant-Leadership*. Copyright © 2009 Margaret Wheatley. Printed with permission of the author. Use of the material in "The True Professional" has been granted by Jossey-Bass, 989 Market Street, 5th Floor, San Francisco, CA 94103.

NOTES

Preface

1. From the last paragraph of Abraham Lincoln's First Inaugural Address, March 4, 1861. Full text at http://www.bartleby.com/124/pres31.html.

2. Herman Hesse, *The Journey to the East* (New York: Picador, 2003), 106.

3. Ninoy Aquino, "The Filipino Is Worth Dying For" (speech, Asia Society, New York, August 4, 1980). Full text at http://www.kylexter.net/2009/04/filipino-is-worth-dying-for-by-benigno.html.

4. From Martin Luther King, Jr., "The Drum Major Instinct." Audio at http://www.thekingcenter.org/.

5. Robert K. Greenleaf, *Servant Leadership: A Journey into the Nature of Legitimate Power and Greatness* (Mahwah, NJ: Paulist Press, 2002), 30.

6. Quoted in Fritz Erpel, *Van Gogh: The Self-Portraits* (New York: New York Graphic Society, 1969), 17.

7. Song of Solomon 8:7, 8 (NRSV).

8. Greenleaf, 27.

9. Viktor Frankl in *Man's Search for Meaning*, http://www.goodreads.com/author/quotes/2782.Viktor_E_Frankl.

Chapter One

1. Robert K. Greenleaf, *Servant Leadership: A Journey into the Nature of Legitimate Power and Greatness* (Mahwah, NJ: Paulist Press, 2002), 23.

2. Nelson Mandela, *Long Walk to Freedom* (Boston: Little, Brown, 1994).

3. Robert D. Enright and Joanna North, eds., *Exploring Forgiveness* (Madison: University of Wisconsin Press, 1998).

4. Juana Bordas in *Reflections on Leadership: How Robert K. Greenleaf's Theory of Servant-Leadership Influenced Today's Top Management Thinkers*, ed. Larry C. Spears (New York: Wiley, 1995), 12.

5. Murray Bowen, *Family Therapy in Clinical Practice* (Northvale, NJ: J. Aronson, 1978).

6. Virginia Satir, *Conjoint Family Therapy* (Palo Alto, CA: Science and Behavior Books, 1964).

7. Martin Luther King, Jr., *A Testament of Hope* (San Francisco: HarperCollins, 1986), 135.

8. Ibid., 139–140.

9. Desmond Tutu, *No Future without Forgiveness* (New York: Doubleday, 1999), 35.

10. Ibid, 253.

11. Ibid.

12. Ibid., 269.

13. James MacGregor Burns, *Leadership* (New York: Harper and Row, 1978).

14. Susan R. Komives, Nance Lucas, and Timothy R. McMahon, *Exploring Leadership: For College Students Who Want to Make a Difference* (San Francisco: Jossey-Bass, 1988).

15. Greenleaf.

16. Bowen.

17. John W. Gardner, *On Leadership* (New York: Free Press, 1990), 116–118.

18. Komives, Lucas, and McMahon, 232.

19. Greenleaf, 20.

20. Ibid., 38.

21. Ibid., 327.

22. M. Ramsey, "A Hermeneutic Phenomenological Investigation of Empathy and Forgiveness in South Africa" (PhD diss., Gonzaga University, 2003).

23. Martin Luther King, Jr., "The Drum Major Instinct." Audio at http://www.thekingcenter.org/.

24. Kahlil Gibran, *The Collected Works* (New York: Knopf, 2007), 268.

Chapter Two

1. K. L. Kirkham, "Teaching About Diversity: Navigating the Emotional Undercurrents" (PhD dissertation Brigham Young University, 1977).

2. Richard Griswold del Castillo and Richard A. Garcia, *César Chávez: A Triumph of Spirit* (Norman: University of Oklahoma Press, 1995), 105.

3. Andrés Irlando (address, K–12 Model Curriculum Team, Los Angeles, June 24, 2001).

4. List of interviews and selection criteria statement in the César Chávez Model Curriculum on the California Department of Education Web site, http://www.cde.ca.gov/.

5. Larry C. Spears, "Service," in *Insights on Leadership: Service, Stewardship, Spirit, and Servant-Leadership*, ed. Larry C. Spears (New York: Wiley, 1998), 15.

6. K. Blanchard, "Servant-Leadership Revisited," in *Insights on Leadership*, ed. Larry C. Spears, 21–28.

7. Retrieved from http://www.greenleaf.org/whatissl/, and found in Robert Greenleaf's original essay *The Servant as Leader* (1970), which can be purchased from the Greenleaf Center for Servant-Leadership at http://www.greenleaf.org/, and is also reprinted in Robert K. Greenleaf, *Servant Leadership: A Journey into the Nature of Legitimate Power and Greatness* (Mahwah, NJ: Paulist Press, 2002).

8. Paulino Pacheco, interview by Ruben Zepeda, August 2001, Santa Maria, CA. All interviews cited in this article are accessible at the California Department of Education César Chávez Model Curriculum Web site, http://www.cde.ca.gov/.

9. Alfred Athie (seventy-three-year-old construction worker and César Chávez's bodyguard), interview in Spanish by Ruben Zepeda, August 2001.

10. César Chávez (speech to students, San Francisco State University, San Francisco, CA, March 30, 1990).

11. M. Moses, "Farmworkers and Pesticides," chap. 10 in *Confronting Environmental Racism: Voices from the Grassroots*, ed. R. D. Bullard (Boston, MA: South End Press, 1993), 161–178.

12. Athie interview:

> He said, "The condition I impose upon the person who is guarding my life is....He must not carry a single weapon...not in any form." I said, "But it can't be. How can we defend you?" "No knives, no pistols, no manner of weapons. If you accept what I am proposing...it has to be without weapons." I said, "And then how?" Chávez replied, "With your body, with intelligence, with observing, but no weapons. I don't accept indolence."

13. Pete Cohen, interview by Ruben Zepeda, August 2001:

> When I was negotiating, he came to Santa Maria two or three times in four years and participated in the negotiations. I think the second time he came, and he saw the particular grower that I was dealing with. After the grower left the room, he said that the guy was a real a——e. He looked at me and in sort of an amazed way, because he was used to dealing with really crappy people, he looked at me and said, "This guy is a real a——e, isn't he?" I guess what I take, more than anything, is what I referred to in the beginning, his was a great and abiding humanity, which again, you don't really find in a lot of people these days.

14. Del Castillo and Garcia, 132.

15. Raul Ceja (UFW leader and organizer), interview by Ruben Zepeda, August 2001.

16. Robert K. Greenleaf, "Servant-Leadership" in *Insights on Leadership*, ed. Spears (New York: John Wiley & Sons, Inc., 1998), 16.

17. Blanchard, 21–28.

18. Pacheco interview.

19. Maria Baca (farmworker, mother, and housewife). Excerpt from interview.

20. Greenleaf, "Servant-Leadership," 19.
21. Baca interview.
22. J. Craig Jenkins, *The Politics of Insurgency: The Farm Workers Movement in the 1960s* (New York: Columbia University Press, 1985), 179.
23. Pacheco interview.
24. Greenleaf, "Servant-Leadership," 16.
25. Dolores Huerta, quoted in del Castillo and Garcia, 73.
26. "Yet, the powerful reputation that Chávez acquired during two decades of organizing migrant fieldworkers is still strong. He is still a figure of moral authority, particularly in the Hispanic and labor communities, and over the years he has burnished that image by frequent exposure. He has marched with casino workers on Las Vegas picket lines, spoken on behalf of gay rights activists at Hollywood dance spots, and he has been arrested in anti-apartheid demonstrations on campuses." *Maclean's,* September 9, 1985, quoted in Pam Morrison, "Cesar Chavez Fights Again," *Los Angeles Times,* September 16, 1996.
27. Mark Shepard, *Gandhi Today: The Story of Mahatma Gandhi's Successors* (Washington, DC: Seven Locks Press, 1987), 124.
28. Del Castillo and Garcia, 176.
29. From Gloria Anzaldúa, *Borderlands: La Frontera, the New Mestiza* (San Francisco: Aunt Lute Books, 1999).
30. Athie interview.
31. Erik Chávez (grandson of César Chávez), interview by Ruben Zepeda, August 2001:

> You got to see him, you got to enjoy his humor, you got to enjoy his comments. He enjoyed a lot of times, because of his generation, and he would scat, "skididobopideboppopbo." That is what he would call each kid, his little "skididobopideboppopbo." It was a joke amongst us, but it was cute. It was adorable, and at that time you don't realize that "skididodabebop" just came out of his mouth. He always had that warm endearing personality. Which for us, it was like, yeah! Then you would hear people say things like, "Your grandfather is a very stern man, he is very difficult, and he is causing a lot of problems." I'd say, "No, no,

no, you all don't understand. He is not causing problems, and he is doing things to help society. He's helping you. He's helping your parents." You are trying to
say all of this when you are only ten years old.

32. Margaret Wheatley, "What Is Our Work" in *Insights on Leadership*, ed. Spears, 348.

33. César Chávez (speech to farmworkers, Delano, CA, 1968), http://www.wccusd.k12.ca.us/stc/Waysofthinking/append/chav ezspeech2.htm.

34. Peter Block, "From Leadership to Citizenship," in *Insights on Leadership*, ed. Spears, 89.

35. Athie interview.

Chapter Three

1. Lao-Tzu (600 BC), *Tao Te Ching*, 17, trans. George Cronk (1999), http://www.bergen.edu/faculty/gcronk/TTC.html.

2. George Bernard Shaw, *Man and Superman* (Cambridge, MA: The University Press, 1903).

Chapter Four

1. Ann Howard and Douglas Weston Bray, *Managerial Lives in Transition: Advancing Age and Changing Times* (New York: Guilford Press, 1988).

2. Joseph L. Moses and William C. Byham, *Applying the Assessment Center Method* (New York: Pergamon Press, 1977).

3. Christopher A. Bartlett and Sumantra Ghoshal, *MIT Sloan Management Review* (Winter 2002).

4. Douglas Weston Bray, Richard J. Campbell, and Donald L. Grant, *Formative Years in Business: A Long-Term AT&T Study of Managerial Lives* (New York: Wiley, 1974), 18–20.

Chapter Five

1. Robert K. Greenleaf, *Servant Leadership: A Journey into the Nature of Legitimate Power and Greatness* (Mahwah, NJ: Paulist Press, 2002), 255.

2. Greg Merten, "Leadership as a Commitment to Personal Development" (speech, Dimensions of Leadership Conference for the Leadership Development Academy of the Graduate School USDA, Washington, DC, 2002), www.solonline.org.

3. Parker Palmer, "Sadness as Moral Virtue" (speech, Greenleaf Center for Servant-Leadership, 2002).

4. Deborah Welch, "Reflective Leadership: The Stories of Five Leaders Successfully Building Generative Organizational Culture" (PhD diss., Union Institute, 1998).

5. Ibid.

6. Ibid.

7. Ibid.

8. Tessa Martinez Pollack, pers. comm., 2002.

9. Welch.

10. Margaret Wheatley, pers. comm., 2002.

11. Don Frick, afterword to *Insights on Leadership: Service, Stewardship, Spirit, and Servant-Leadership*, ed. Larry C. Spears (New York: Wiley, 19987), 357.

12. Greenleaf, 317–18.

13. Welch.

14. Ibid.

15. Ibid.

16. Doc Lew Childre and Howard Martin, *The HeartMath Solution: The Institute of HeartMath's Revolutionary Program for Engaging the Power of the Heart's Intelligence* (San Francisco: HarperSanFrancisco, 2000).

17. Gregg Levoy, *Callings: Finding and Following an Authentic Life* (New York: Three Rivers Press, 1998).

18. Greenleaf, 12.

19. Humberto Maturana and Gerda Verden-Zöller, "The Biology of Love" in *Focus Heilpadagogik*, ed. G. Opp and F. Peterander (Ernst Reinhardt: Munich/Basel, 1996). Available at

http://www.lifesnaturalsolutions.com.au/documents/biology-
of-love.pdf.

20. Teilhard de Chardin, *Toward the Future* (London: Collins, 1975), 86–87.

21. Greenleaf, 41.

Chapter Six

1. Sharif Abdullah, *Creating a World That Works for All* (San Francisco: Berrett-Koehler, 1999), 19–20.

2. Robert K. Greenleaf, *The Servant as Leader* (Indianapolis: Greenleaf Center, 1990), 7.

3. John E. Foley, "Ethics and Civility in Collective Decision Making," April 1995, 2.

4. Based upon the work of Ken Wilber in *A Brief History of Everything* (Boston: Shambala, 2001).

5. Stanislav Grof, *The Ultimate Journey* (Ben Lomond, CA: MAPS, 2006), 317.

6. William Glasser, *The Control Theory Manager* (New York: Harper, 1994).

7. Greenleaf, 72.

8. Ibid., 76.

9. Ernest Laszlo, *You Can Change the World* (New York: Select Books, 2003), 4.

10. Ibid., 7.

11. Greenleaf, 27.

12. Ibid., 76.

13. Don Alverto Taxo, *Friendship with the Elements* (Ecuador: Ushai, n.d.), 56.

14. Bill Bottum with Dorothy Lenz, "Within Our Reach: Servant-Leadership for the Twenty-first Century" in *Insights on Leadership: Service, Stewardship, Spirit, and Servant-Leadership,* ed. Larry C. Spears (New York: Wiley, 1998).

Chapter Seven

1. Stephen Mitchell, *Tao Te Ching* (New York: Harper Collins, 1988), chap. 27.
2. As cited in Lance Secretan, *Insight: What Great Leaders Do* (Hoboken, NJ: Wiley, 2004), 93.
3. Mitchell, chap. 17.

Chapter Eight

1. Robert K. Greenleaf, *The Servant as Leader* (Indianapolis: The Greenleaf Center, 1990), 7.

Chapter Nine

1. Wayne Dyer, *The Power of Intention* (Carlsbad, CA: Hay House, 2004).
2. Danah Zohar and Ian Marshall, *Spiritual Capital: Wealth We Can Live By* (San Francisco: Berrett-Koehler, 2004).
3. Robert K. Greenleaf, *Servant Leadership: A Journey into the Nature of Legitimate Power and Greatness* (New York: Paulist Press, 1977).
4. Don Frick and Robert K. Greenleaf, *A Life of Servant Leadership* (San Francisco: Berrett-Koehler, 2004).
5. Greenleaf, 15–16.
6. Ibid., 141.
7. Marshall Goldsmith and Howard Morgan, "Leadership Is a Contact Sport," *strategy+business* (Fall 2004).
8. Institute for Policy Studies and United for a Fair Economy, 14th Annual CEO Compensation Survey, *The Staggering Social Cost of U.S. Business Leadership* (Washington, DC, 2007).
9. Zohar and Marshall, 42.
10. Greenleaf, 15.
11. George Arliss, www.leadershipnow.com.
12. Chris Argyris, *Reasons and Rationalizations: The Limits to Organizational Knowledge* (New York: Oxford University Press, 2006).

13. Greenleaf, 13.

14. Pablo Freire, *Pedagogy of the Oppressed* (New York: Continuum, 1995).

Chapter Ten

1. Robert K. Greenleaf, *The Servant as Leader* (Indianapolis: Greenleaf Center, 1990), 7.

RECOMMENDED READING

Autry, James A. *The Servant Leader*. Roseville, CA: Prima Publishing, 2001.

Block, Peter. *The Answer to How Is Yes: Acting on What Matters*. San Francisco: Berrett-Koehler, 2001.

————. *Community: The Structure of Belonging*. San Francisco: Berrett-Koehler, 2008.

————. *Stewardship: Choosing Service over Self-Interest*. San Francisco: Berrett Koehler, 1993.

DePree, Max. *Leadership Is an Art*. New York: Doubleday, 1989.

————. *Leadership Jazz*. New York: Doubleday, 1992.

————. *Leading without Power*. San Francisco: Jossey-Bass, 1997.

Ferch, Shann Ray, ed. *The International Journal of Servant-Leadership*. Spokane: Gonzaga University; Indianapolis: Spears Center, 2005–2009.

Greenleaf, Robert K. *Advice to Servants*. Indianapolis: Greenleaf Center, 1991.

————. *Education and Maturity*. Indianapolis: Greenleaf Center, 1988.

————. *Have You a Dream Deferred?* Indianapolis: Greenleaf Center, 1988.

————. *The Institution as Servant*. Indianapolis: Greenleaf Center, 1976.

————. *The Leadership Crisis*. Indianapolis: Greenleaf Center, 1978.

————. *My Debt to E. B. White*. Indianapolis: Greenleaf Center, 1987.

————. *Old Age: The Ultimate Test of Spirit*. Indianapolis: Greenleaf Center, 1987.

————. *On Becoming a Servant-Leader*. San Francisco: Jossey-Bass, 1996.

————. *The Power of Servant-Leadership*. San Francisco: Berrett-Koehler, 1998.

————. *Seeker and Servant*. San Francisco: Jossey-Bass, 1996.

————. *Seminary as Servant*. Indianapolis: Greenleaf Center, 1983.

————. *The Servant as Leader*. Indianapolis: Greenleaf Center, 1990.

————. *The Servant as Religious Leader*. Indianapolis: Greenleaf Center, 1982.

————. *Servant Leadership: A Journey into the Nature of Legitimate Power and Greatness*. New York: Paulist Press, 1977.

————. *Servant Leadership 25th Anniversary Edition: A Journey into the Nature of Legitimate Power and Greatness*. Mahwah, NJ: Paulist Press, 2002.

————. *The Servant-Leader Within*. Mahwah, NJ: Paulist Press, 2003.

————. *Spirituality as Leadership*. Indianapolis: Greenleaf Center, 1988.

————. *Teacher as Servant: A Parable*. Indianapolis: Greenleaf Center, 1987.

————. *Trustees as Servants*. Indianapolis: Greenleaf Center, 1990.

Hesse, Hermann. *The Journey to the East*. New York: Noonday Press, 1992.

Jaworski, Joseph. *Synchronicity: The Inner Path of Leadership*. San Francisco: Berrett-Koehler, 1996.

Jones, Michael. *Creating an Imaginative Life*. Berkeley: Conari Press, 1995.

Koestenbaum, Peter, and Peter Block. *Freedom and Accountability at Work: Applying Philosophic Insight to the Real World*. San Francisco: Jossey-Bass/Pfeiffer, 2001.

McGee-Cooper, Ann, and Gary Looper. *The Essentials of Servant-Leadership: Principles in Practice*. Waltham, MA: Pegasus Communications, 2001.

SanFacon, George. *A Conscious Person's Guide to the Workplace*. Victoria, BC: Trafford, 2007.

Showkeir, Jamie, and Maren Showkeir. *Authentic Conversations: Moving from Manipulation to Truth and Commitment*. San Francisco: Berrett-Koehler, 2008.

Spears, Larry C., ed. *Insights on Leadership: Service, Stewardship, Spirit, and Servant-Leadership*. New York: Wiley, 1998.

———. *Reflections on Leadership: How Robert K. Greenleaf's Theory of Servant-Leadership Influenced Today's Top Management Thinkers*. New York: Wiley, 1995.

Spears, Larry C., and Michele Lawrence., eds. *Focus on Leadership: Servant-Leadership for the 21st Century*. New York: Wiley, 2002.

———. *Practicing Servant-Leadership*. San Francisco: Jossey-Bass, 2004.

Spears, Larry C., and Paul Davis, eds. *The Human Treatment of Human Beings*. East Lansing, MI: Scanlon Foundation, 2009.

———. *Scanlon EPIC Leadership*. East Lansing, MI: Scanlon Foundation, 2008.

Wheatley, Margaret J. *Leadership and the New Science Revised: Discovering Order in a Chaotic World*. San Francisco: Berrett-Koehler, 1999.

———. *Turning to One Another*. San Francisco: Berrett-Koehler, 2002.

Williams, Lea E. *Servants of the People: The 1960s Legacy of African American Leadership*. New York: St. Martin's, 1996.

Zohar, Danah. *Rewiring the Corporate Brain*. San Francisco: Berrett-Koehler, 1997.

INDEX

191

CONTRIBUTORS

Editors and Contributing Authors

Shann Ray Ferch, PhD, Professor of Leadership, Gonzaga University

Shann Ray Ferch is married to Jennifer and is the father of three great girls, Natalya, Ariana, and Isabella. As a poet and prose writer, his work has appeared in some of the nation's leading literary venues including *McSweeney's*, *Narrative Magazine*, *StoryQuarterly*, *Best New Poets*, and *Poetry International* (www.shannray.com). *American Masculine*, his collection of short stories, won the Bakeless Prize and appears with Graywolf Press. As professor of leadership with the internationally renowned PhD program in Leadership Studies at Gonzaga University (www. gonzaga.edu/doctoral), his emphasis is on how servant-leadership honors collective responsibility and self-transcendence across the disciplines. He holds a PhD in psychology, a dual MFA in poetry and fiction, and is a member of the Academy of American Poets. Dr. Ferch has served as a research psychologist with the Centers for Disease Control, the United States Government, and is a systems psychologist in private practice. The editor of *The International Journal of Servant-Leadership*, Dr. Ferch, in collaboration with senior advisory editor Larry Spears, publishes essays and scholarly work dedicated to the wisdom, health, autonomy, and freedom of others. Shann grew up in Alaska and Montana, and lived on the Northern Cheyenne Reservation in southeast Montana. He currently lives in Spokane, Washington.

Larry C. Spears, President and CEO, The Larry C. Spears Center for Servant-Leadership

Larry C. Spears is president and CEO of the Larry C. Spears Center for Servant-Leadership, established in 2008 (www.spears center.org). From 1990 to 2007 he served as president and CEO of the Robert K. Greenleaf Center for Servant-Leadership. Spears has previously served as director or staff member with the Greater Philadelphia Philosophy Consortium, the Great Lakes Colleges Association's Philadelphia Center, and with the Quaker magazine, *Friends Journal*. Spears is also a writer and editor who has published hundreds of articles, essays, newsletters, books, and other publications on servant-leadership. Dozens of newspapers and journals have interviewed him, including *Fortune*, the *Indianapolis Business Journal*, *Philadelphia Inquirer*, *Washington Post*, and *Advancing Philanthropy*. A 2004 television broadcast interview of Spears by Stone Phillips on NBC's *Dateline* was seen by ten million viewers. Larry is the creator and editor of a dozen books on servant-leadership, including the best-selling *Insights on Leadership*. Larry serves as the senior advisory editor for *The International Journal of Servant-Leadership* (2005–present), and he teaches graduate courses in servant-leadership at Gonzaga University. In 2010 he was appointed servant-leadership scholar at Gonzaga University. Among several honors, Spears was the recipient of the 2004 *Dare-to-Lead Award* given by the International Leadership Network, and the 2008 Community Leader Award given by DePauw University. Larry has thirty years of experience in organizational leadership, entrepreneurial development, nonprofit management, and grant writing, having envisioned and authored thirty successful grant projects.

Contributing Authors

James A. Autry is an author, poet, and consultant, whose work has had significant influence on leadership thinking and has been a vital force in promotion of the arts. Before taking early retirement in 1991 to pursue his present career, Autry was senior vice-president of the Meredith Corporation and president of its magazine group. At the time of his retirement, Autry was regarded as one of the most successful and respected magazine publishing executives in America. In 1989, he was named Magazine Executive of the Year by the Association for Education in Journalism and Mass Communications. His book, *Love and Profit: The Art of Caring Leadership*, won the prestigious Johnson, Smith, and Knisely Award as the book that contributed the most to executive thinking in 1992. Autry was appointed by President Carter in 1979 to serve on the national advisory committee for the White House Conference on Families, and in the mid-1980s was president of the Institute for the Advancement of Health. Autry lives in Des Moines with his wife, Sally Pederson, the former lieutenant governor of Iowa.

Lane Baldwin, a musician and songwriter, has toured the world and recorded with dozens of artists. His servant-led band Deeper Blues preaches a message of community to share the pain and the healing power of the blues. As a business consultant, he promotes servant-leadership and humanistic management practices to others while using them to guide his own companies. As a writer, poet, and speaker, Lane offers a message of living in harmony and finding fulfillment in the service of others. As a person, he's just trying to be the best human being he can be. More information is available at www.lanebaldwin.com.

Peter Block's work is about empowerment, stewardship, chosen accountability, and the reconciliation of community. He is the recipient of the first-place 2004 Members' Choice Award by the Organization Development Network, which recognized *Flawless Consulting* (1999) as the most influential book for organization development practitioners over the past forty years. He helps create workplaces and communities that work for all. His books offer an alternative to the patriarchal beliefs that dominate our culture and his work brings change into the world through consent and connectedness rather than through mandate and force.

Olle Blohm is a Stockholm-born writer and the coauthor of *Hostmanship: The Art of Making People Feel Welcome* and *The Welcoming Leader: The Art of Creating Hostmanship*. A practical philosophy on the art of welcoming, hostmanship is based on six foundations: serving, responsibility, wholeness, caring, knowledge, and dialogue. For more information about the ideas behind hostmanship visit www.hostmanship.com.

Virginia Duncan Gilmore served as vice-president of sales and customer satisfaction for her family owned manufacturing business, Kaytee Products, until 1997. In the last ten years she has founded the Center for Spirituality and Leadership at Marian College in Fond du Lac, Wisconsin. She also founded the Sophia Foundation to invite community collaboration through the principles of servant-leadership in support of a vision of "caring community." The foundation has awarded grants of over $450,000 to encourage courageous action for systemic change to support transformational growth for women and children in vulnerable situations. In addition, Virginia is a speaker, educator, facilitator, spiritual guide, and an advocate for peace and understanding in her community and in our world.

Jan Gunnarsson is a Swedish inspirational author and speaker with more than thirty years of experience from the service industry. After several years of working directly with guests, he has been engaged in travel destinations, hotels, and special attractions in managing, marketing, and business development roles including president of Scandinavian Tourism USA and head of development of the Swedish Travel and Tourism Council. Jan speaks on all aspects of welcoming people, as customers and partners, as co-workers and as oneself. He works with clients in all fields of society throughout the world. Jan is the coauthor of *Hostmanship: The Art of Making People Feel Welcome* and *The Welcoming Leader: The Art of Creating Hostmanship*. For more information about the ideas behind hostmanship visit www.hostmanship.com.

Jeff McCollum, MS organizational development, is an organizational development practitioner based in Phoenix. He consults in the areas of organizational development and leadership development. Before establishing his own consultancy, Star*Thrower Associates, he worked for AT&T, Warner-Lambert, and Pfizer. He is a former member of the Greenleaf Center for Servant-Leadership's Board of Trustees.

Joel Moses has been actively involved in assessing and developing leadership talent for over forty years. At AT&T he was responsible for establishing and directing its Advanced Management Potential Assessment Center and directed its management selection and development research unit. From 1989 to 2006, Dr. Moses was president and managing director of the Applied Research Corporation, a firm specializing in identifying leadership talent. He recently joined the Valtera Corporation as a senior practice fellow. A frequent contributor to the literature on assessment centers, his book, *Applying the Assessment Center Method* (with Bill Byham) was one of the first describing this method. Joel has an MBA (CUNY) and a PhD (Baylor University). A fellow of the Society of Industrial and Organizational Psychology, he received its prestigious Professional Practice Award in 2000.

María D. Ortíz obtained her graduate education from Brigham Young University and The Union Institute and University respectively. Her teaching and academic career spans nearly twenty years and includes teaching organizational development, organization theory, ethnic studies, critical thinking, and facilitating various service learning projects within her course assignments. While teaching in the community colleges in California, Dr. Ortíz conducted research to develop and write successful grant projects to support first-year-college experience for at-risk students. Her work and practice are consistently renewed and informed by organizational behavior and living systems theory, and the persistent voices of a community of practice.

George SanFacon is the author of *Awake at Work* and *A Conscious Person's Guide to the Workplace*. From 1983 to 2004, he served as director of the housing facilities department at the University of Michigan, where he helped pioneer implementing the council-of-equals model.

Jamie Showkeir has a long-standing relationship with the Greenleaf Center for Servant-Leadership, where he has provided training and consulting services. He is the founding partner of henning-showkeir & associates, a consulting firm focused on sustaining change in organizations by creating workplaces where people find meaning and purpose as the primary means for achieving business results. Jamie was president of the Autism

Society of Michigan and served as dean of the School for Managing and Leading Change. He is the coauthor, with his wife Maren, of *Authentic Conversations: Moving from Manipulation to Truth and Commitment*, published by Berrett-Koehler.

Maren Showkeir joined henning-showkeir & associates as a partner in 2005, and is involved in all aspects of managing the business and working with clients. She began her career in the media and worked for more than twenty-five years as a journalist, editor, and manager at major-market newspapers in Arizona and Florida. She believes that the actions of effective leaders are authentically grounded in service, which influenced her leadership and management style throughout her career. She is co-author with her husband, Jamie, of *Authentic Conversations: Moving from Manipulation to Truth and Commitment*, published by Berrett-Koehler.

David Wallace is a husband, father, linguist, and a student of servant-leadership. He has worked in several Central Asian countries, most recently as the coordinator of a New Testament translation project in the Kyrgyz language. He holds a BA in music from Bethany University and an MA in organizational leadership from Azusa Pacific University.

Deborah V. Welch has twenty-five years of experience in the field of psychology and leadership, and works with leaders in colleges, school districts, small businesses, corporations, and family foundations. Dr. Welch is also a faculty member at Capella University, mentoring dissertation research, and teaching masters- and doctorate-level courses such as performance enhancement, group facilitation, and the psychology of leadership. Her consulting work focuses on leadership development, coaching, and board development. She is the founder of Reflective Leadership Global.

Margaret Wheatley is president emeritus of the Berkana Institute, and an internationally acclaimed speaker and writer. She has been an organizational consultant and researcher since 1973 and a dedicated global citizen since her youth. Her first work was as a public school teacher and urban education administrator in New York, and a Peace Corps volunteer in Korea. She also has been associate professor of management at the Marriott School of

Management, Brigham Young University, and Cambridge College, Massachusetts. Margaret's path-breaking book, *Leadership and the New Science* was first published in 1992, and has been translated into twenty languages. This book is credited with establishing a fundamentally new approach to how we think about organizations. It is a standard text in many leadership programs, and has won notable awards, including "Best Management Book of 1992" in *Industry Week*, "Top Ten Business Books of the 1990s" in *CIO Magazine*, and "Top Ten Business Books of All Time" by Xerox Corporation. A new edition was published in 1999, significantly revised, updated, and expanded. The video of *Leadership and the New Science*, produced by CRM films, has also won several awards.

ABOUT THE LARRY C. SPEARS CENTER FOR SERVANT-LEADERSHIP

The mission of the Larry C. Spears Center is to create a more caring and serving world through the understanding and practice of servant-leadership. It has a primary emphasis upon the publications by Larry Spears and Robert K. Greenleaf.

The Spears Center is a 501(c)3 charitable organization that seeks to fulfill its mission through its emphasis upon servant-leadership in relation to the following program areas and key initiatives:

Servant-Leadership Publications
Global Network
Personal Development
Best Organizational Practices
Higher Education
Events & Personal Presentations
Universal Bridge for Servant-Leaders of Differing Faiths and
    Philosophies
Council of Equals Initiative

The Larry C. Spears Center for Servant-Leadership, Inc.
329 Garden Grace Drive
Indianapolis, IN 46239
317-416-8218
www.spearscenter.org

Servant Leadership [25th Anniversary Edition]
A Journey into the Nature of
Legitimate Power and Greatness
Robert K. Greenleaf

A classic work on leadership for business men and
women, government leaders and all persons
in positions of authority.

0-8091-0554-3   Hardcover
978-1-61643-042-9   PDF

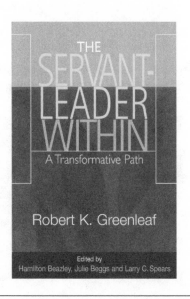

The Servant-Leader Within
A Transformative Path
Robert K. Greenleaf; edited by Hamilton Beazley,
Julie Beggs, and Larry C. Spears

Combines in one volume classic works on
servant-leadership and its relationship to the art
of teaching and the act of learning.

0-8091-4219-8   Paperback

To Be a Servant-Leader
Stephen Prosser

Based upon or inspired by biblical texts,
To Be a Servant-Leader examines the main
characteristics or principles of leadership.

978-0-8091-4467-9   Paperback

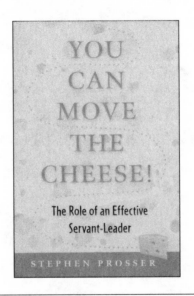

You Can Move the Cheese!
The Role of an Effective Servant-Leader
Stephen Prosser

Identifies five key people propositions, practiced by
enlightened companies, and invites leaders to become
purposeful, principled, resolute and exemplary
as they transform their places of work
and the lives of their followers

978-0-8091-4640-6   Paperback

Seven Pillars of Servant Leadership
Practicing the Wisdom of Leading by Serving
James W. Sipe and Don M. Frick

Offers a skills-oriented approach to acquiring the
most critical competencies of effective servant leadership,
all without overlooking matters of the heart
and soul that make it all worthwhile.

978-0-8091-4560-7   Paperback
978-1-61643-031-3   PDF

A Servant Leader's Journey
Lessons from Life
Jim Boyd

A series of reflections on coping with a fatal disease,
but also an insightful examination of
living and dying by a widely acclaimed authority
on organizational leadership.

978-0-8091-4568-3   Paperback

Servant Leadership Models for Your Parish
Dan R. Ebener

Servant Leadership Models for Your Parish explores the
practice of servant leadership in a church context.
It presents seven behaviors practiced by leaders
and members in high-performing parishes and
provides real-life examples of these practices.

978-0-8091-4653-6 Paperback

The Gratitude Factor
Enhancing Your Life through Grateful Living
Charles M. Shelton, PhD

Explores the significance of gratitude for one's personal and spiritual life, offering a unique blend of the latest research and practical strategies and exercises to foster a grateful heart.

978-1-58768-063-2   Paperback

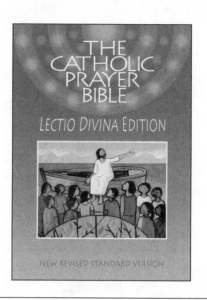

The Catholic Prayer Bible (NRSV)
Lectio Divina Edition
Paulist Press

An ideal Bible for anyone who desires to reflect
on the individual stories and chapters of just one,
or even all, of the biblical books, while being led
to prayer though meditation on that biblical passage.

978-0-8091-0587-8   Hardcover
978-0-8091-4663-5   Paperback